Extraordinary North Dakotans

ERLING NICOLAI ROLFSRUD

by the author of . . .
> THE TOP DRAWER
>
> GOPHER TAILS FOR PAPA
>
> LANTERNS OVER THE PRAIRIES
>
> CHURCH ETIQUETTE FOR THE LAYMAN
>
> WHITE ANGAKOK
>
> BROTHER TO THE EAGLE
>
> THE BORROWED SISTER

Extraordinary
North Dakotans

by
ERLING NICOLAI ROLFSRUD

published by
LANTERN BOOKS
ALEXANDRIA, MINNESOTA

Copyright, 1954

by

ERLING NICOLAI ROLFSRUD

All rights reserved

Except for brief quotations embodied in reviews, no part of this book may be reproduced in any form without written permission of the author.

First Printing

Printed in the United States of America
by Lakeland Color Press, Brainerd, Minnesota

To
ELDA VAN DYKE DODGE

The Author

Preface

The lecture was concluded. As the Junior High School students were leaving the auditorium, a Senior strolled by and inquired of a Freshman, "What was your program about?"

"About interesting people in North Dakota."

"About interesting people in *North Dakota!*" exclaimed the older boy with caustic sarcasm, "*That* must have been *very* interesting!"

Overhearing this conversation, I, the visiting lecturer, was reminded of a McKenzie County youth who yearned to flee the North Dakota prairies so that he could live where there were people worthy of his pen.

In an empty granary bin, that farm youth wrote his first novel — a novel with a most enchanting California setting. That he had never lived beyond his Dakota hills did not deter this lad from writing with confidence. The novel, however, failed to enchant any editor or publisher.

A neighbor was the plank-riding preacher whose story you will find in this book, but the youth saw in that neighbor only a staid cleric, surely no subject for *his* art. It was years before his vision cleared sufficiently that he beheld about him folks of book-hero stature.

This is his fourth book about people of his native state.

There will be restitution for the author's early lack of vision. if his books awaken some fledgling writer—with granary-bin perspective — to the realization that many other prairie biographies and novels wait to be written.

— ERLING NICOLAI ROLFSRUD

Acknowledgements

This book of miniature biographies is an outgrowth of research done by the author for Lyceum Lectures on "Extraordinary North Dakotans" and delivered in North Dakota schools in 1952-1953.

So many people contributed to the factual fabric of the stories related in these pages that it would be impractical to list them all here. The bulk of biographical information was obtained through interviews and correspondence, and newspaper accounts. The author expresses his sincere thanks to all who assisted with factual data.

The following books provided information:

> *Jim's Western Gems* by J. J. Somers
> *Land of the Golden Grain* by Patrick Donan
> *North Dakota Medicine* by James Grassick
> *Tales from Buffalo Land* by Usher L. Burdick
> *Ten Stubby Fingers* by Ida Prokop Lee
>   by Elizabeth Preston Anderson
> *The Real Thing, The Ruling Hand* and *Old Glory*
>   by Budd Reeve
> *Under the Prairie Winds* (in manuscript)

Grateful acknowledgement is made for special help given by the following persons:

> Miss Elsie Jane Wheeler, Portland, Oregon
> Miss Grace Watkins, Fargo
> Mrs. Robert Soderholm, Worthington, Minnesota
> Mr. Russell Reid, Miss Margaret Rose and Mrs. Martha Wetmore of the North Dakota Historical Society
> The staff of the North Dakota State Library Commission
> Miss Jean Dunlop, librarian, The Fargo *Forum*
> Miss Blanche Lynch and Mr. Robert Cory of the Minot *Daily News*
> Miss Clara A. Richards, librarian, Masonic Grand Lodge Library, Fargo
> Miss Nellie R. Swanson, librarian, State Teachers College, Minot

Table of Contents

Preface		VII
Acknowledgements		VIII
1 - Introduction		1
2 - The Biggest Boy in the World	Jimmie Janousek	3
3 - The Giant of Frog Point	Carl Rauk	5
4 - The Smallest Pioneer	Edward Laning	6
5 - King Whiskers	Hans Langseth	7
6 - Big-Prairie Cleric	I. J. Buckneberg	9
7 - Squatter Governor of North Dakota	Dennis Hannafin	14
8 - The Sage of Buxton	Budd Reeve	19
9 - Agent of Almighty God	Josephine Grinnell	22
10 - Champion of Buffalo Hunters	Frederick "Doc" Zahl	24
11 - Hanging Party Host	Hans Thorpe	28
12 - Blue-Blood Purveyor of Butter	John Sutherland Sinclair	30
13 - Maid-in-Waiting to Queen Victoria	Marie Downing Williams	32
14 - Cowboy Doctor and Talented Daughter	V. H. Stickney / Dorothy Stickney	36
15 - Liver-Eating Johnson		47
16 - Gunnysack Bill		48
17 - Mustache Maud		49
18 - Flying Cloud	Frank B. Zahn	52
19 - Red Tomahawk	Marcellus Red Tomahawk	55
20 - Brother to the Sioux	Frank B. Fiske	58
21 - Fiddler, Regardless	Ted Anderson	62
22 - Badlands Artist	Einar Olstad	63
23 - Rising Bear, Schoolteacher	Charles W. Hoffman	68
24 - Long-Haired Morgan	Morgan Spencer	79
25 - The Undiscovered Poet of the West	J. J. Somers	80
26 - Lazarus	Mark L. Hanson	84
27 - Wrong Side Up	John Christiansen	85
28 - Crusading Lady	Elizabeth Preston Anderson	89
29 - North Dakota's First Hello Girl	Bella Thomson Webster	96
30 - Tree-Tops Klingensmith	Florence Gunderson Klingensmith	98
31 - "Dinna Forget Your Peat"	James Grassick	102
32 - Captain of the Minnie-H	Edward Heerman	108
33 - The Golden-Haired Reverend Goldie		110
34 - Battling Country Lawyer	Gudmundur Grimson	111
35 - Correspondence Study Crusader	T. W. Thordarson	119
36 - Prairie-Town Merchant	M. A. Johnson	127
37 - Horation Alger of the Prairies	Harold Schafer	136

38 - *Mister Give Away*	Harry F. McLean	140
39 - *Three-Facet Artist*	Paul Broste	143
40 - *Gold Star Bandmaster*	Clarence S. Putnam	147
41 - *Collector of Butterflies*	Emil Krauth	151
42 - *Schoolwoman of the Red Maxwell*	Minnie J. Nielson	155
43 - *Creator of Prairies Pictures*	Ida Prokop Lee	161
44 - *North Dakota's Ace Athlete*	Casper Oimoen	168
45 - *World's Champion Miniature Writer*	James W. Zaharee	171
46 - *Telle, Woodcarver*	Thelma Rudser	175
47 - *Crochet Specialist*	Eugene B. Nelson	180
48 - *Other Hobbyists*	Louis Braaten	183
	Archie Brown	
	Frank Johnson	
	Henry Klebe	
	H. J. Rustad	
49 - *The Clever-Handed Kotschevars*	Mr. and Mrs. H. J. Kotschevar	185
50 - *Artist in a Henhouse*	Joseph Messer	187
51 - *Rural School Godmother*	Leila C. Ewen	192
52 - *Rosemeade Lady*	Laura Taylor Hughes	199
53 - *Ole, the Hermit*	Ole Olson	205
54 - *Whittler of Birds*	Thomas Hansen	207
55 - *Indomitable Artist*	Grace Layton	210
56 - *Three Maids and a Mission*	Janet M. Smaltz	214
	Marge Hurst	
	Lucille Holtan	
57 - *Champion of the Shackled*	Anne H. Carlsen	219
58 - *Lady Under the Sod*	Anna Fisher	227

Extraordinary North Dakotans

1

A PIONEER editor in western North Dakota once declared the climate in the state to be so invigorating, and the soil so fertile that if one should plant a spike in the ground in early spring, by fall that spike would have grown to be a 6-foot crowbar.

While New Englanders or other unenlightened folk might consider such a claim with lifted eyebrow, Dakota homesteaders, inspirited by their Patrick Donan's paean, *The Land of the Golden Grain,* would have accepted the editor's statement without question.

This Colonel Patrick Donan once was hired by a railway company to write advertising literature designed to attract settlers to the Dakota prairies. As a blurb writer, Donan was seventy-five years ahead of his time; even the super adjectives of Hollywood hucksters leave the reader unmoved after he has perused a pamphlet authored by this spellbinder in 1883. Consider two samples:

> *Let mythology tell of the garden of the Hesperides, and mystical Elysiums; let poets rave of their Vales of Tempe and Cashmere; let Egypt boast of her wondrous, God-watered Valley of the Nile, Italy of her olive-crowned slopes, and France of her vine-clad hills; but in our glorious New Northwest, there is a valley fairer and more fruitful than them all . . . a land fair enough to tempt the angels in their flight to pause and wonder if here a new and better Eden has not been formed and roofed with sapphire skies.*

And North Dakota climate, that special prairie commodity so greatly disparaged by Easterners who have never crossed the Appalachians was adequately treated by Donan:

> ... People who have come here to die of bronchitis and consumption have lived to become glowing embodiments of sound strength, with throats like firemen's trumpets and lungs like blacksmith's bellows. The howling blizzards of which outside worldlings delight to prate, blow all miasma and contagion from Dakota's favored plains and valleys, and breathes new life into delapidated nostrils. The enfeebled parson from down East, whose wheezy tones scarce suffice to stir the flies that crawl over the bald pates of his dozing elders and deacons, is soon able, not only to keep his hearers awake, but almost to arouse, as with a forty-donkey-power bugle blast, the sheeted sleepers in the churchyard; and the frail, ethereal housewife whose tremulous whispers were unheard beyond the ruffles of her muslin cap, can scold her husband or her boys in steam-calliope soprano notes that resound a square away.

When, in February of 1883, Donan addressed citizens at Dayton, Ohio, his Pied Piper call was heard with wonderment as he promised those who chose to follow him to Dakota Territory that there they would find potatoes growing "as big as beer-kegs, at the roots of every tuft of prairie grass," also "cabbage heads of congressional and senatorial size."

2 The Biggest Boy in the World

IT comes, therefore, as no surprise to native North Dakotans to learn that in this "Land of No. 1 Hard" have grown some native sons who gave living proof that Donan spoke the sober truth. There was, for instance, one born on a farm near Veseleyville who was acclaimed "The Biggest Boy in the World."

Although neighbor folks in Walsh County accepted Jimmie Janousek as a rather commonplace wonder, Bob Ripley excitedly reported his "discovery" to the world in his *Believe It or Not* columns.

At birth, Jimmie weighed 16 pounds. When he was in the first grade in a Sander District 58 rural school, his teacher, Miss Glenna Sander, had difficulty fitting Jimmie to a school desk because at seven, he weighed 235 pounds.

Problems in regard to facilities for Jimmie increased with passing years. By the time he was fourteen years old and in the eighth grade, he had grown to such size that he could not get inside an automobile, and had to be transported in a farm pickup truck. When he checked his weight it was by typical North Dakota scales at a grain elevator. At fourteen, he tipped the grain elevator beam at 587 pounds.

As an eighth grade pupil, he had a rather trim waistline; it measured 73 inches. His mother made all his clothes; she used five yards of material for a pair of trousers, and the same yardage for a shirt.

The last time this good-natured Big Boy was weighed, the reading was 720. Unofficial estimates have put his maximum weight at over 800.

Jimmie Janousek of Veseleyville,
"The Biggest Boy in the World"

Carl Rauk

Photo by courtesy of
F. Cooper, Portland

Circuses made attractive offers to the Janousek family for Jimmie's exhibition, but they consistently rejected all offers.

A boy of good humor, Jimmie was a favorite in his community. He was only nineteen when he died in 1946.

3 The Giant of Frog Point

*H*OMESTEADERS near the once-thriving but now extinct metropolis of Frog Point evinced in Carl Rauk the stimulating effect of North Dakota climate. When he arrived in the Red River Valley in March of 1878, he was merely a husky young man and of no extraordinary dimensions. But, after settling in Donan's "land of swift and magnificent growth," Carl grew and grew until he weighed 530 pounds and reached 6 feet 6 inches in height.

He lived in his four-room house not far from his parents' claim. His willow chair, his bed, and his buggy were especially built to his proportions.

For all his bulk, Rauk was an active man. He owned and operated a steam threshing rig. Once when he was threshing on the Peter Bye farm, the crew — consisting of a dozen men — went in ahead of him to supper. When Carl came and took his assigned place at the table, the floor joists not only creaked, but they cracked — and the thirteen men and the supper table spilled into the cellar.

For a short time, Carl hired out to a dime museum in Minneapolis. The occupation of merely exhibiting himself proved much too boresome; he was always falling asleep on the job.

At Grand Forks one time a carnival show fat man boasted to the crowd of his incomparable avoirdupois. Along came Carl Rauk. Up he got on the fat man's stage, surveyed the braggart disdainfully as he remarked, "So you think you are somebody, eh?" Standing alongside Rauk, the carnival man was both dwarfed and chagrined.

While Jimmie Janousek was the only member of his family to attain phenomenal size, Carl Rauk had three big brothers — Ole, Lars, and Christian who weighed 310, 275, and 250 pounds, respectively. Of Carl's four sisters, Marget was something of a discredit to the heavyweight family, for the most she ever attained in weight was a scant 165 pounds. Now 92 years of age, Mrs. Marget Rauk Cooper lives near Buxton.

Carl Rauk died on his thirty-fifth birthday, October 8, 1893, and was buried at Belmont Cemetery not far from his homestead.

4 The Smallest Pioneer

AS the exception that proves the rule, Edward Laning of Killdeer is believed to have been the smallest pioneer in North Dakota. He was 4 feet 7 inches in height, and weighed 75 pounds. Of wiry build, he was reported able to outwork most men of even twice his size.

Laning homesteaded in Dunn County in 1906, and died at Fayette in 1936. He fervently clung to the belief that Dunn County would some day produce great gas and oil wells. At the time of his death, he was seventy-five years old, and had the distinction of being the smallest and oldest bachelor in the state.

5 King Whiskers

LENGTHY evidence of the remarkable accomplishments of North Dakotans was provided by the late Hans Langseth of Barney.

Born in Norway, he came to America in 1876, a young man eager to build a fortune in the New Land. He farmed in Iowa and next in Minnesota, then settled permanently in Richland County in 1901.

Prosperity did not long elude him in the "paridisean valley of the Red" where Donan claimed "marvelous soil pours forth almost spontaneously from 30 to 40 bushels of barley, from 50 to 100 bushels of oats, and from 20 to 400 bushels of potatoes, to the acre, and everything else in proportion." Hans Langseth farmed and he speculated in real estate; he amassed a considerable acreage, and owned stock in a couple of banks.

It was not his material possessions, however, that brought this farmer the attention of an admiring public.

Like most gentlemen of his day, Hans grew a beard. But *his* beard became a phenomenal one — and that due to the fact that Hans Langseth was an observing fellow.

He had noticed that the hair on a man's face would break off at waist length, but that which grew from under the chin was of much greater durability. So when Hans was thirty years old, he decided to find out just how long chin whiskers could grow.

It wasn't long before those luxurious strands were getting in the way. Industrious farmer that he was, Hans could not let the experiment handicap his activities. So he wrapped the whisker ends around a little stick, put the coil into a protective bag, and tucked the whole inside his vest.

Hans Langseth, "King Whiskers"

Well, the whiskers grew and grew and grew, and after attaining nearly half a century of growth, the coil inside Langseth's vest was so large that, spare man though he was, he bore a paunch.

When the beard reached 17 feet and 4 inches in length, its owner joined Ringling Brothers Circus to display the "longest beard in the world." The contract was of very short duration, however. Langseth's feelings were hurt when people viewed with skepticism a beard that was so genuine. Furthermore, his chin got sore — for in every crowd would be some smart-aleck who would reach over and jerk the end of the beard as it lay displayed in full-length glory upon a long table.

Hans, therefore, made precipitate return to North Dakota where honest folk respect the genuine article. Once, though, he went to Sacramento, California to compete in a "Days of '49" whisker contest. As might well be expected, Langseth quickly shamed all contestants and was crowned "King Whiskers," and presented with a gold slug suitably engraved for the occasion.

At the time of Langseth's death in 1927, the beard had attained a length of 18 feet 6 inches.

6 Big-Prairie Cleric

FRESH out of seminary, the young minister regarded, with enthusiasm, his 10,000-square-mile Dakota parish. From Palermo west to the Yellowstone Valley, from the Blue Buttes in McKenzie County and north to the Canadian border, there was no other Lutheran pastor save himself when the Reverend Ingvald J. Buckneberg established headquarters at Ray, in July of 1905.

His first ecclesiastical appointment was a wedding ceremony near Hofflund, 20 miles distant. After pedaling his bicycle thither over the prairie hills and coulees, he concluded that a speedier and less arduous mode of conveyance must be obtained without delay.

On the way back, then, he stopped to confer with a horse trader who was offering a team of "lively" horses for sale. A span of mettled ponies, young Pastor Buckneberg shortly was persuaded, exactly filled his need to reach a maximum number of settlers in a minimum of time.

But were these lively horses, he queried the trader, safe for a preacher's use? As to that, the man hedged, he could not judge, since he was not a clergyman himself. Nor could he give any sort of guarantee. He would, however, drive the team for the Reverend on his first trip with them.

The credulous tenderfoot paid for the span of wild Indian broncos. And it was not until months afterward that he learned that these lively horses had run away with the trader, pitched him from the buggy, scattered it over the hills, and so unnerved the man that when he finally caught the runaways he kept them fast in the barn, until the day of their sale.

So, the deal concluded, the trader and a helper proceeded to harness the spirited ponies to a buggy which the Reverend also purchased.

Buckneberg noted that the men approached the team with extreme caution and that they exchanged confidential and subdued words as they led the steeds out of the barn and toward the buggy. Too, the trader stood at the horses' heads and kept firm grip on their bridles while his assistant gently prodded them toward the buggy tongue and hooked the tugs. But the Reverend climbed in, and settled upon the buggy seat.

With surpassing alacrity the trader sprang in beside him. And no less swiftly the broncos shot off across the prairie. Jutting rocks, prairie dog hills and gopher mounds — all were but flashes to the new owner as he clung to the pitching buggy seat.

"Are you sure you can stop these horses?" he asked the driver.

"Oh, certainly," between gritted teeth, the trader replied, "we just drive them square against the barn wall and they stop."

They reached Ray in record time, and headed "square against" the barn which Buckneberg had rented. Confronted with the wall, the beasts came to an unwilling stop.

The trader, assisted somewhat by Buckneberg, got the heaving team unhitched and inside the barn. Taking his leave, then, he suggested. "Better you have a man help when you hitch them horses, Rev'rund."

The young Reverend thanked him for his advice. Then he considered the fact that there was no hay, that some must be run down, and that job must be accomplished by use of the team needing it.

He succeeded in getting Ed Emerson, who operated a local eating place, to go along out to see a farmer who had hay for sale.

As before, destination was reached in record time. And, happily, without incident. On the start back, though, Emerson's leap onto the buggy seat was in effect like a released trigger as the impatient horses lunged away. Seconds only and cook and cleric were sprawled in a potato patch, the lively horses had divorced themselves from the buggy, and hid themselves in an old straw barn.

The clergyman, the cook, and the farmer gleaned buggy parts from the prairie grass, fitted the parts together, and reunited the broncs with the fractured buggy. Then, the farmer, with friendly concern, warned, "Pastor Buckneberg, you better get rid of those broncs before they get rid of you!"

The take-off and return trip were accomplished without mishap. The next morning Buckneberg surveyed his fractious horses with a stubborn confidence in their worth. He resolved to learn to handle them alone, and immediately.

Eager to be about his pastoral calls, he put his satchel in the buggy. He brought one of the broncos from the barn, and secured it to a stout post just outside the barn door. Then he brought out the second pony, tied it beside its mate. He drew the buggy up behind them, and hitched them to it. With smooth haste he unfastened them from the post and got himself into the buggy.

The fleet-footed span carried him safely on that first pastoral call, and raced him over his extensive parish on many another. Not always, it must be confessed, were the trips without upset or runaway. Buckneberg came to enjoy his travels behind them, but as for the lively horses, it seemed not to matter to them whether he accompanied them or not. Yet, because of their speed and endurance he was able, in only a few years, to organize close to twenty congregations.

In time he secured a homestead near Charlson, in McKenzie County, married and had a family.

His place was on the south side of the tawny Missouri while most of his scattered congregations were north of it. There were weeks during the spring thaw and again during fall freeze-up when his spirited Indian ponies could not get him across "Old Muddy" in the sleigh, nor could the ferry transport him and the team and buggy. At such times, there was only one way that was at all possible for a man to get across the river. The ferryboat operator of that time, Mr. Octave Geertz — now living near Keene — testifies that although several men attempted to cross that way, none ever accomplished the feat except the Reverend Ingvald J. Buckneberg.

The big prairie cleric rode a plank across the wide Missouri.

It happened in the fall of 1908. Buckneberg had been away for some time holding daily meetings among those congregations across the river, and on his way a heavy snow fell. By the time he reached the river it had a thin coat of ice, and the ferry had stopped running for the season. He tried the ice but it was not yet thick enough to support his weight. He was desperately homesick, and his young wife, twelve miles beyond those glazed waters anxiously awaited his return.

On the opposite banks of the river two great timbers had been upraised, and from the top of each was fastened a heavy steel cable which swayed across the river..During the summer, this cable was used in steering the ferryboat. In the fall and spring when it was not possible for the mail carrier to get across, the cable served in transporting the mail bags over the river.

To accomplish this, an 8-foot plank was slung by pulleys so that it dangled about three feet below the cable. To each end of this horizontal plank a rope was attached so that when the mail bags had been secured to the top of the plank, it could be pulled across the river with the rope.

"A man" — the desperate cleric resolved within himself — "could ride that plank across the river!"

He shivered in the cold night fast settling down. He regarded the box of groceries and small suitcase of clothes at his feet; and next, the fourteen-year-old boy who was accompanying him home for the winter.

He made plain to the boy the hazards of getting astride that dangling plank 50 feet above the river's surface. There was no one to draw the plank across by the rope attached to its end; Buckneberg would have to pull himself and the boy across by a hand-over-hand pull on the steel cable.

The lad — whose name, regrettably, is not recorded — was game. So man and box, boy and suitcase, moved up and up the short lengths of pole nailed ladder-wise to the great timber.

Cautiously, the pastor got himself astride the plank. He fastened the grocery box and the suitcase to the middle of the plank. Then the plucky boy crept out upon the swaying conveyance.

For the first half of the trip across the pulleys rolled easily; the cable sagged toward the center. The second half of the trip was an uphill pull. And often the preacher broke his hand-over-hand rhythm to rest.

Boy and man did not indulge in conversation as they straddled that plank and inched toward the home side. Nor did their eyes stray from the home shore for a glance at the river far below.

The opposite great timber reached, they crawled gratefully to the ground, then made their way through snow drifts to a homesteader's place where they got a horse and sled to cover the remaining miles.

His ministerial days ended, Buckneberg farmed for a stretch of years in McKenzie County. When he retired, he went to Helena, Montana where his only daughter lived, and there, on October 27, 1948, he died.

7 Squatter Governor of North Dakota

THE "Squatter Governor" of North Dakota, Dennis Hannafin, was born in County Kerry, Ireland, in 1835. When "Denny" was ten, his family embarked for the promised land of America. During the journey, the father died out on the Atlantic; so, young Denny became the "man of the family."

At Buffalo, and later at Attica, New York, the Irish lad worked as bootblack, newsboy and farm hand to help support his mother and sisters. When fifteen, having secured a grade school education, Denny left his family and set out for the West.

He found employment with a Central Illinois railway construction company. Then in July of 1862 he enlisted with the 75th Illinois Infantry, and, on rendering distinctive service in the Battle of Perrysville, was commissioned a lieutenant. Following several battle engagements, he marched with Sherman to the sea. Mustered out of service at Chicago, the strapping young adventurer headed farther west.

He became general trader, working in advance of railway construction — first with the Union Pacific, later with the Northern Pacific, as it extended its way through Minnesota and Dakota Territory.

The Reverend I. J. Buckneberg

Dennis Hannafin, "Squatter Governor of North Dakota"
North Dakota Historical Society photo

Budd Reeve, "The Sage of Buxton"
North Dakota Historical Society photo

He was one of the first settlers of Moorhead, Minnesota. While living there, he learned that a party of St. Paul capitalists, cooperating with the NP's land company, was setting out to locate a town where the NP would cross the Missouri River.

Denny decided it would be smart to get hold of that townsite land before the capitalists did. Always a man of persuasive tongue, he forthwith fired the ambitions of four other young fellows, and the five scurried west across the Dakota prairies to reach the centuries-old buffalo crossing where the NP railway bridge now spans the Big Muddy. Each of them squatted on an 80-acre tract, and settled down to await the arrival of the capitalists.

The St. Paul men duly arrived and, of course, found the coveted location already taken. Denny and his pals scorned — one time too many — the lucrative offers made by the St. Paul men and so the townsite planners decided that their town of Edwinton (later Bismarck) could be located just as advantageously a mile from the bank of the river.

(Denny's claim was located just west of the present-day Episcopal Church. Some years later, at one of the many times when Dame Fortune had turned her fickle back on him, he sold it for a small price.)

Life on the claim soon proved boring for the itchy-footed Irishman. In September, 1873, accompanied by three other frontiersmen — John Warn, Jack Kale and Jesse McCoy — he crossed the Missouri to do some private prospecting along the proposed route of the NP.

The Sioux Indians, jealously guarding their hunting grounds, had, the previous summer, attacked NP surveyors and run off with cattle at Fort Abraham Lincoln. Consequently, orders had been issued that no one should go west of the Missouri without military escort.

Ignoring this mandate, Denny's party set out across the Missouri bottom lands. But when they arrived at a bluff where the city of Mandan now is, they spied below them a band of scalp-happy Sioux. The four prospectors flattened themselves on the ground and spurted gun fire in the direction of the Indians. Denny's strategic position a-top the bluff soon discouraged the redskins, and the encounter stimulated the whites to forge further into the Sioux domain.

They scouted as far west as Green River before turning back toward Denny's river-bank claim. Near the present site of Sims, they came upon an outcropping of lignite coal — and ever since, Denny has been given credit by many as the first to discover coal in North Dakota.

He was exulting over his find when he caught sight of a party of Sioux braves covertly circling the place. Denny felt his scalp tingle. He needed no persuasive eloquence to set the other men at helping dig breastworks in the crown of the hill. The four prospectors worked fast and effectively. Daily, for the next two weeks, they were attacked by the Indians — but were safe behind the fortification of sod which they constantly strengthened. Thus was Fort Hannafin established.

Game was plentiful in the vicinity of this fort; abundant fuel was at hand for winter months. So Jack Warn made the sod-walled fort his home for the next seven years.

Back to the civilized side of the Missouri, Denny, at the first election, found himself chosen as county attorney. He rejected the honor since he felt that he should be admitted to the bar before accepting the responsibilities of such an office. At the first term of court held in Bismarck, Judge Hudson examined Denny, and admitted him to the bar.

While Hannafin spasmodically practiced law for some years, and was occasionally associated with a prominent St. Paul attorney, he found law far too tame a mistress. He frequently went off on long tramps, his provisions and a bed roll strapped upon his back. It was not uncommon for him to walk from Bismarck to Fargo in the dead of winter. Sometimes he hiked right on to St. Paul. In 1874 he tramped from Sioux City, Iowa to Elk Point, Dakota Territory to attend a Democratic convention.

It was politics that finally ensnared Denny's interest and held it for the rest of his life. After North Dakota had become a state, Hannafin was always in Bismark to provide counsel — without charge — to legislators and other officials of state. Until the end of his days, he never missed a session of the legislature although he held no political office.

His vigorous comments on the political arena and his sarcastic evaluations of various Capitol personages were frequently publicized in the Bismarck *Tribune* and other state newspapers. He made summary disposal of Bismarck attorneys as: "Seven-Up lawyers — moving from block to block with big safes — nothin' in 'em but a squirrel skin, a pair of socks and a *Tribune* with the delinquent tax list in." Taxes aroused his ire: "In the first place, taxation is too general and is becoming too familiar with men who have never exhibited a desire to cultivate its acquaintance . . . No man should be compelled to pay taxes unless he owns a railroad, rides in palace cars or runs for office. If the Constitution will fix it so that every man who walks is exempt from taxation we will raise tougher and better men, and first-class pedestrians will be as numerous as Farmers' Alliance statesmen." For Minneapolis — where there were "too many sun-cured politicians" to suit him, he proposed the publication of a new daily, one to be dubbed *Twin City Tail Twister*.

When the "Third House," an organization of legislative employees, held its first meetings, members elected Hannafin their honorary chief and gave him the title of "Squatter Governor." The title was his for the rest of his life.

He devised his own coat-of-arms: "A rampant wild cat perched upon a roaring lion confronted by an infuriated tiger, the whole beautifully mounted upon the crashing fragments of a magnificent earthquake."

One of the most colorful figures to frequent the Capital during the early decades of the state, Dennis Hannafin died at Bismarck, November 5, 1917. A speculator who several times barely missed a fortune, the Squatter Governor was ever a good loser. He had a host of friends, many of them among the notables of the state and nation.

8 The Sage of Buxton

FROM down the road the villagers heard the clangor of a cow bell. So incessant was the sound, they wondered if some bossy were in flight with a dog at her heels.

But no cow was to be seen, and no dog. When the hectic sound got the louder, housewives went out on door steps and their menfolks came out into the dusty streets to cock a suspect ear in the direction of a remarkable vehicle that was approaching.

As this equipage neared, villagers beheld a small log cabin surmounted on a wagon chassis and drawn by horses. Above this cabin rippled the Stars and Stripes.

The politically-enlightened of the village nodded knowingly. That unique conveyance, the autumn of 1898, could bear none other than the Democratic candidate for Congress: Budd Reeve.

From one Red River Valley town to another, Reeve campaigned — summoning his audiences with the bonging cowbell. Once his clanging had attracted a crowd, he spoke with eloquence and great conviction. He attacked the evils of the free silver policy, praised the ideals of the "old-line" Democrat — elaborating, in that connection, on the symbolism of his campaign equipment: the pioneer log cabin, the American flag, and his traveling companion — a live eagle.

But despite his original campaign methods, and the good will his sincerity always left in his wake, this "Sage of Buxton" failed to obtain a seat in Congress.

Born on a pioneer Indiana farm, in 1842, Reeve was several years a Hoosier schoolmaster, then turned to the study of law, and, at 26, was admitted to the bar. As a Minneapolis lawyer, he prospered, and invested in real estate in that city.

In 1880, he was detailed to select a suitable site for a railroad station, and the town of Buxton thereby came to be. While on this mission, he purchased a farm for himself, shortly after located there, and became manager of the Buxton Townsite Company.

Always a man of great enthusiasm, Budd informed prospective buyers of real estate that the day would come when "Buxton will be as well known as Rome." He pointed out that while Horace Greeley urged the young man to go west, he failed to tell the young man just where to locate. This missing detail of information, Reeve gladly supplied, and further counseled the young man: "If you are old enough to have one, it would be a pious idea to bring a wife along."

While Budd Reeve farmed, he conceived a rather unorthodox philosophy based upon a mystic manipulation of numbers. These philosophical tenets he expressed in several of the books he wrote and published. In *The Ruling Hand* he announced that God had "come down and filed on a farm claim" in North Dakota. The legal description of this particular property — Section 25, Township 148, Range 51, Buxton, Traill County — was ascertained by the mystic numbers. Temporary tenant on this farm was Budd Reeve, himself.

The Real Thing by Budd Reeve, Himself provided the reader with poetry, some of which was inspired by the author's "long, lean, lank, tall, grim, gaunt sow." Poetic discourses by the sage of Buxton covered divers subjects including "My Name Is Not Carnegie, But I Freely Give To The Public." On the back cover of the volume, the prospective reader learned that the book "can only be had from the author personally . . . The reason for this is, that unless a man has a monopoly of some kind nowadays, he is considered a 'back number'."

Reeve's patriotic fervor found release in *Old Glory* wherein he purported to show "God as the head and founder of the United States, and the flag, as purely and distinctly His."

The sage of Buxton invented the Budd Reeve Seed Cleanser, a contrivance he described as a "Trust Buster That

Talks For Itself." This farm machine had a "social side" and was also a "home circle harmonizer." Of this the inventor himself brought proof: "I am seventy-one years old and weigh one hundred and ten pounds, but I can clean seed grain in the house when the piano is playing, surrounded by books and pictures on the wall, whether it is forty below zero or one hundred in the shade, better and quicker than the strongest man can do it with any other machine."

A man of great courage in championing whatever he believed to be right and good, Reeve espoused public causes in such books as *What I Think After Thinking by Budd Reeve, Himself* and *Washington's Temperance Victory*. In this latter book, Reeve, a prohibitionist, elaborated on the story of General Washington's capture of the drunken Hessian hirelings the Christmas of 1776.

Budd's worth to his adopted state was proved in 1893 when the University of North Dakota faced the tragedy of closing its doors because of insufficient funds. Reeve hurried to Minneapolis and St. Paul where he canvassed his friends — men among the officials of banks, and of railway and grain concerns. He returned with enough money to keep the University in operation until the legislature was able to make necessary appropriations.

Budd Reeve died at his Buxton farm in 1933, at the age of 91.

9 Agent of Almighty God

THE coroner's jury did not deliberate long before it delivered a most bizarre verdict: that George Grinnell "came to his death through an act of Almighty God, by the hand of His agent, Josephine Grinnell."

Back of that verdict is the story of the woman who was the "agent of Almighty God."

Josephine was born at Like-a-Fish-Hook Village in 1860, the daughter of Beaver Woman, an Hidatsa Indian, and Charles Malnorie, a Frenchman who owned a trading post at old Fort Berthold.

High-spirited and intelligent, Josephine was the first of the Indian students to leave the Fort Berthold Indian Reservation and seek further training at Hampton Institute in Pennsylvania. Her mother, fearful that the girl might be kidnaped and never return, strongly opposed Josephine's venture after more of the white man's education.

So Josephine left secretly. The night before she was to leave, she hid her clothing down at the boat landing. The next morning, she stole from her home, and filled with trepidation, boarded a river steamer.

She returned from three years at Hampton full of learning and with a store of interesting tales with which to regale her folks and friends. Her favorite topic was the fancy clothes worn by army officers' wives traveling on the river steamers. Particularly intriguing to her had been the ladies' slippers. In describing them, she would indicate with her fingers the length of the heels and would say, "Heels this much!"

To Fort Berthold, accompanying a military train from Fort Snelling, Minnesota, came the adventuresome George

Grinnell. He remained to hunt game along the Missouri, and to establish a woodyard to supply fuel to river steamers. He was at once attracted to the beautiful and accomplished Josephine Malnorie and they were married.

From the start, life with the tempestuous former army spy was rugged experience for Josephine. Under the influence of liquor, her husband would subject her to indignities that her breeding could not tolerate. After establishing a saloon of his own at Williston, he became increasingly abusive.

The arrival of children made no difference in him. One extremely cold winter day when the oldest child wandered away from home, Josephine ran to her husband's saloon to summon aid in finding the boy. But the drunken husband, always resentful of the proud woman's resistance to becoming a squaw-wife, saw this as an opportunity for vengeance.

He bristled savagely when Josephine implored the men at the bar to help find the child she adored. "I'll kill the first man that goes out to look for that boy of hers," he vowed.

Among the men in the group was George Newton, famed buffalo hunter. He looked Grinnell full in the face and said, "Then you've got me to kill."

Grinnell's bluff had been called. If he shot Newton, he knew the other men would quickly gather a mob to deal him western noose-justice.

Newton stalked out of the saloon, and shortly returned the boy to his mother. But the incident served to fan the flame of Grinnell's resentment toward Josephine.

By 1888, four children had been born to the Grinnells: three boys, George, John and Charles, and a baby girl, Ellen.

One day Grinnell came home from his saloon, savagely abusive. To protect herself, Josephine, with baby Ellen in her arms, ran to a nearby field where several men were working.

On horseback, the drink-crazed Grinnell pursued her. He charged up to her, and tried to strike her with the butt of his pistol. Too drunk to maintain his balance, he toppled from the saddle and fell upon Josephine.

The men, afraid of Grinnell's gun, would not risk interference. The desperate mother, her baby gripped in one arm, struggled against her raging husband.

Suddenly George Grinnell lay still.

He had always worn around his neck a leather watch thong with a sliding knot. With her one free hand, Josephine had grasped this thong and strangled him to death.

A coroner's jury was immediately summoned to the spot, and quickly reached the unusual verdict which absolved Josephine Grinnell of all guilt in the death of her husband.

For the young mother, it was the beginning of brighter days. She returned to her people on the Fort Berthold Reservation where she found work as a cook at Fort Stevenson, and later she moved to Elbowoods.

Before her death at Elbowoods in 1945, this much-respected and well-loved mother saw the fruition of her dreams for her children. The baby daughter she had gone to such drastic means to protect grew into beautiful womanhood, and was married in a ceremony at the Elbowoods Mission church. And the daughter of this Ellen not only grew up to wear "heels this much" but, having inherited her grandmother's great beauty, was elected homecoming queen at the Minnesota college from which she was graduated.

10 The Champion of Buffalo Hunters

MOST Americans assume that "Buffalo Bill" Cody was the greatest of all buffalo hunters. But that title belonged instead to one Zahl who later served as the first treasurer of Williams County.

Cody was a showman; he attracted attention to himself through his Wild West Shows and he wrote a book about his own exploits.

"Doc" Zahl, on the other hand, was a modest man. While the tales of his hunting prowess were told again and again around many a western camp fire, this man who became an almost legendary hero never publicized himself.

The greatest number of buffalo that Buffalo Bill ever shot in one stand was 69; Zahl's comparable record was 120.

An orphan boy of 12, Frederick Randolph Zahl, with his younger brother Frank, came to America from Germany in 1869. In New York City, they had to wait for one day in the railway station before they could continue on their way; but it was during this enforced wait that they first learned about Buffalo Bill, the current hero of all red-blooded American boys. When they got on the train that was to take them to their elder brothers at Morris, Minnesota, they had decided on a career: they would be buffalo hunters.

For the next four years, however, the buffalo hunting had to be postponed while the two boys worked on farms the greater part of the year, and hunted muskrat and mink during the winter months. But when Doc was sixteen, he and his brother headed west with a wagon team — and rifles.

Arrived at Fort Sully, they decided to stay for a while, and try their luck hunting buffalo.

On their first day out, the Zahl brothers discovered a herd of buffalo grazing along a creek just a few miles west of the Fort. Fired with excitement, they stole within easy shooting distance of the prairie monarchs. Doc took careful aim, fired on a huge bull. Wounded, the bull thundered away across the prairie. The entire herd followed in wild stampede.

The boys returned to the Fort empty-handed; for them, Buffalo Bill was all the greater hero.

At camp that night, Doc met an old half-breed buffalo hunter and to him reported his day's disappointing experience. The grizzled veteran listened sympathetically, but shook his head over Doc's aiming at the buffalo's head. That was no way to shoot a buffalo!

The animal should be shot in the paunch, in a small space near the hip, explained the halfbreed. Then it would become intensely ill and would lie down and die without disturbing the herd. But if it were shot in other parts of the body where the wound caused stinging pain, it would become frightened and bolt away — with the rest of the herd following.

The next afternoon, Doc and his brother came upon a large herd of the bison several miles west of the Fort. Stealthily and against the prairie wind, they maneuvered within rifle range. Doc aimed for that small area near the hip bone of a bull and fired. He watched amazed as the bull lay down. Heedless, the herd continued to graze. Now the younger Zahl leveled his rifle and sighted at the spot just below the back and to the fore of the hip bone, and the bullet spat from the gun. A second buffalo settled down upon the prairie grass. In just a short while, a dozen of the bulls lay upon the ground, and the undisturbed herd went on feeding.

The two youths decided they had felled enough buffalo to keep them busy skinning the rest of the day. They advanced in sight of the herd, and the buffalo charged wildly away.

At Lead that fall, Doc began to hunt buffalo for a living while Frank got a job in a hotel. Remembering the counsel of the half-breed, Doc hunted with success.

When summer came, they were hired to bury the soldiers who had fallen at the Battle of the Little Big Horn. Come fall, they were both on the trails of buffalo migrating southward for the winter. For a time, they operated a woodyard on the Yellowstone River — a work more remunerative than that of hunting buffalo whose hides now sold for only a dollar apiece. But despite this, the lure of the buffalo did not dim for the two.

Doc's fame for an unerring marksmanship grew. Ranchers, river men, woodhawks, cowboys and nimrods recounted the adventures of this man who could keep four skinners busy where few men could use two skinners. Wealthy men from the East eagerly employed him as scout for their hunting parties. He took Teddy Roosevelt on his first buffalo hunt (and years later was a White House guest when Roosevelt was President).

In 1882, Doc was appointed Deputy U.S. Marshall and served in that capacity for several years. The same year, he and his brother invested their savings in a hunters' hotel at the junction of the Musselshell and Missouri rivers. This was in territory crossed by the buffalo on their annual fall migration. Their first year at the hotel, the Zahls did a profitable business, providing lodging and supplies for the increasing number of buffalo hunters.

In the fall of 1883, hundreds of men arrived in Montana to engage in the sport of shooting buffalo — men eager to return East with a shaggy-haired trophy. The Zahl hostelry was crowded with men ready for the buffalo which usually reached that area in late September. Doc and his brother readily extended full credit for needed supplies; they would be repaid when the hunt was over.

September passed. Not a buffalo appeared.

October days dragged by for men who had often beheld the spectacle of hill and prairie covered with a dark sea of buffalo. Before the month ended, many of the discouraged hunters returned East for no buffalo had yet come down the centuries-old route from the Canadian prairies.

In late December, Doc and his brother were left alone at their outpost, their accounts uncollected, their property worthless — for never again were the monarchs of the prairie to thunder and rumble across the hills and buttes, down prairie valleys to winter in the warm grasslands of the south. Never again would the herds return with spring to the vast feeding grounds of the north. Suddenly, that fall of 1883, had come the inevitable penalty for the slaughter waged increasingly since the middle of the century.

Stunned, the Zahl brothers went to Terry, Montana Territory, and there opened a trading store, also invested in cattle. They engaged in various enterprises together until 1888, when Frank went back to Morris, Minnesota to live. Doc spent two years at Fort Buford, supplying the military post with game which he hunted; he also hauled Fort supplies from Bismarck — using sixteen mules on a jerk line.

He next moved to Williston where he served as the first county treasurer in Williams County. He operated a sales barn and meat market at Williston, later a ranch near Zahl (named in his honor), and he helped establish a chain of six banks in the northwestern part of the state. He died at Zahl on February 10, 1918.

In his buffalo-hunting days, Doc became acquainted with famous Indians such as Rain-in-the-Face, Sitting Bull, Gall, White Bull and Crow King. He knew General George Custer, and he was a personal friend of General Nelson A. Miles who pursued the defiant Sioux until they were quartered on Indian reservations.

11 Hanging Party Host

IN early September, 1900, a man sat in the Minot jail writing invitations to his friends and acqaintances to come to his own hanging party. On Sheriff W. J. Carroll's official stationery, Hans Thorpe wrote these invitations with a flourishing hand, and embellished them with crude drawings.

These hanging-party invitations were not wholly the gesture of hospitality for the prospective host received for the most of them funds for his supply of tobacco, candy, and the "red-eye" in which he "rejoiced."

On the dismal morning of September 14, in response to Thorpe's gruesome overtures, a considerable number of people were admitted to an enclosure on the southern outskirts of Minot. The sky was dark with clouds, and the ground soggy from a night of drizzling rain.

Outside the enclosure was a much larger crowd that had been drawn by morbid curiosity. They punched out knot holes, and even whittled peep holes in the thick boards of the wall.

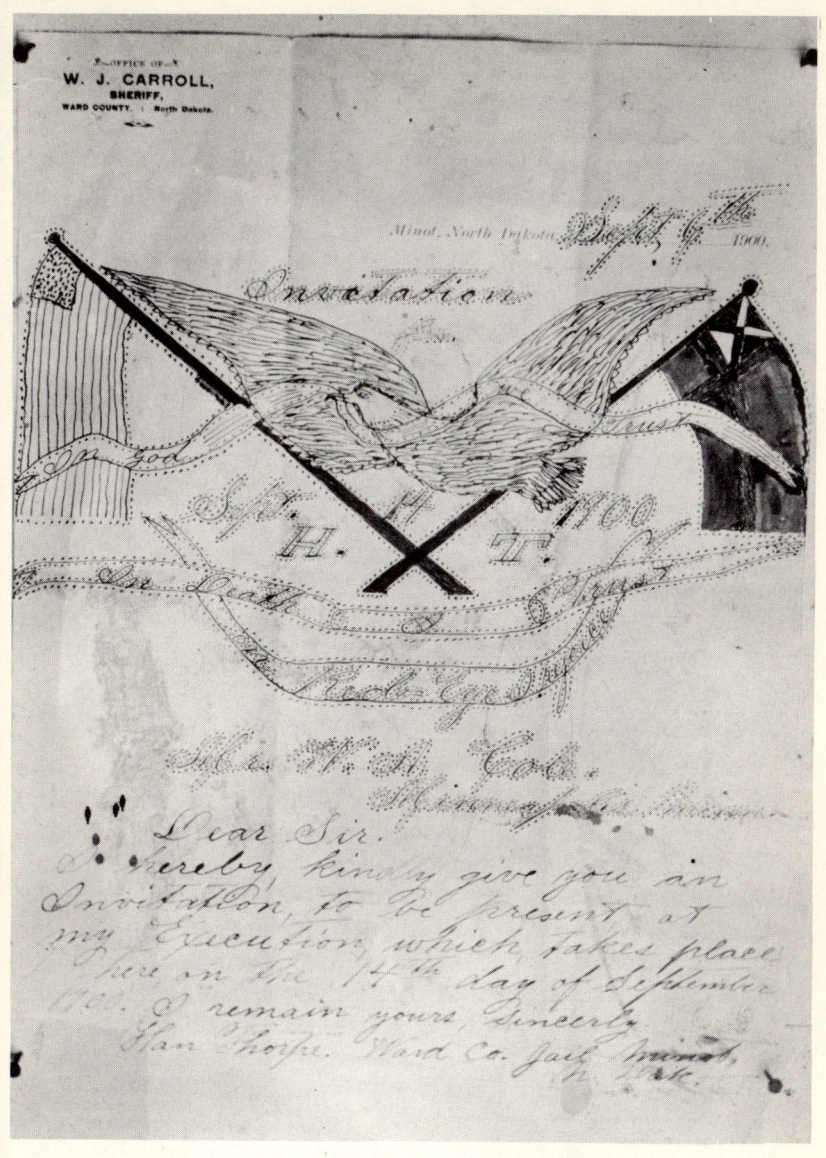

Photo of an invitation to Hans Thorpe's hanging party

Photo by courtesy of Bob Cory, Minot

Little compassion was displayed for the man who was to be hanged. The confessed murderer of his wife, he was callous, and he was cocky.

When led to the scaffold that Judge William Murray had constructed, Hans Thorpe walked stiff-backed—a half-smoked cigar between his teeth, and a smile upon his lips. Erect on the scaffold, he told his guests that he had been insane from jealousy the day he killed his wife. He made some light joke with Marshall McClure, editor of the Minot *Optic*, then stepped onto the trapdoor.

When, at 6:30 that morning, Hans Thorpe dropped to his death, he became the first and last man ever legally hanged in Ward County.

12 *Blue-Blood Purveyor of Butter*

ALMOST all North Dakotans have heard of the spectacular French nobleman, the Marquis de Mores, who owned a ranch and built a meat-packing plant at Medora — where his chateau still stands—and who was acquitted of murder in one of the most dramatic court trials in the history of the state. Few North Dakotans, though, have ever heard of the unassuming thrice-titled Scotsman and descendent of Robert Bruce who drove a buckboard and delivered butter to Lakota townspeople.

This nobleman, John Sutherland Sinclair, had lived on his Nelson County farm for several years before his neighbors discovered that he was actually Lord Beridale of Scotland, and Baronet of Nova Scotia, that he owned an ancient castle, and had a right to a seat in Parliament. It was while he was delivering butter that he inherited the third title, that of Earl of Caithness in northern Scotland.

Only his genteel manners and the quality of his impeccable attire hinted of the fact of his noble lineage. A special accent of his courtly appearance was a bright red silken sash. But in giving his name he used no other title than "Mr."

Arrived in North Dakota in 1884, Sinclair established himself on his 3040-acre Beridale Farm 6 miles northeast of Lakota. He erected imposing buildings, one of them a creamery. In that pre-milking machine day, he had a herd of 55 dairy cows producing about 50 pounds of butter daily.

He shipped most of his butter to Montana markets, and delivered the rest personally to private customers in Lakota. With a team of his fine horses hitched to his buckboard, this Lord Beridale, Baronet of Nova Scotia, and seventh Earl of Caithness, brought butter to the back doors of Lakota homes. It was his habit to stop on his way to town, to inquire of his farm neighbors whether he might perform some errand for them while he was in Lakota.

A large crew of men was necessary to operate the dairy business, to care for a stable of thoroughbred horses, and to till the large grain fields. Many of his workers came from Scotland, their transportation paid for them by the Earl.

A platform a-top the granary served as a lookout from which Sinclair, with field glasses, could view his entire farm and watch the progress of field work. Here, in the early spring, he could see his 30 mules, 4 to a gang plow, turning over the soil. Through the growing season, he would frequently mount the platform to survey his greening acres, to observe the large-scale hay making. In harvest time he spent much time driving his buckboard over the fields, bringing meals and refreshment to his crew.

In 1905, John Sutherland Sinclair sold his Beridale Farm and Lakota neighbors honored him with a farewell banquet. He returned to Scotland, and after making some improvements on his estate in Aberdeenshire, came back to this continent. For a time he lived in the Peace River territory of Canada, then went to California where he served as secretary of a copper mining corporation.

He lived quietly at the Balboa Hotel in Los Angeles, for three years. Following injuries in a traffic accident, he died and was buried at Forest Lawn. At the time of his death, there were only three persons in California who knew that he was a thrice-titled Scotch nobleman.

13 Maid-in-Waiting to Queen Victoria

WERE we given the fantastic choice, most of us would prefer a castle to a North Dakota log cabin home. But not so was it with a certain Rolette County farm woman.

Marie Downing renounced the splendors of Windsor Castle to become the bride of a homesteader, thus to live in a small cabin and experience the rigors of pioneer life on the prairie. Not only did she learn to keep house, but she also took a place in the field along with her husband. Once, when it chanced that he was ill and unable to work, this former maid-in-waiting to Queen Victoria of England, harnessed two colts to a mower and cut a hundred tons of prairie hay which she sold to a livery stable at Rolla. And never did she regret her choice — not even when she found it necessary to help her husband rear forty stacks of wheat. Just being the wife of her beloved Harry Williams, dirt farmer, more than compensated for the life of pomp in a palace.

Eight years Marie Downing had stood daily beside the imperious Empress, anticipating her slightest wish or desire. Eight years she had given intimate, personal service in the royal household — sealing the Queen's own mail, shopping for Her Majesty, helping Her Royal Highness to dress for state occasions — after bringing fabulous jewels from vaults to place upon the Sovereign's person. Eight years she was the favorite personal attendant — witnessing along with his-

John Sutherland Sinclair,
the Earl of Caithness

Photo courtesy of
Mrs. E. J. Taylor, Bismarck

Marie Downing Williams

toric affairs, incidents in the private life of the Queen and Prince Consort Albert and their nine children. In eight years she was the recipient of many costly gifts not only from the British monarch but also from the Queen's close friend, the Empress Eugenie of France.

For two years, Marie Downing implored Queen Victoria to release her from her service so that she might go to America to join her sweetheart. After she gained the promise, she twice was packed and ready to take the next ship across the Atlantic, but was called back into service because her successor had proved unsatisfactory.

Harry Williams had served English royalty first as a page boy, then as a butler. In his 28th year he had emigrated to what Queen Victoria called "savage America." For five lonely years he waited for his bride to come.

When finally Marie reached New York City, customs inspectors detained her, charging that she had more trunks than she had "declared." Such proved to be the case. But happily it developed that the extra trunks had been sent by Queen Victoria — and all were filled with treasures from the royal household!

On January 1, 1887, Marie Downing reached Minnewaukan, the railroad point then nearest Rolla. Harry Williams was there waiting to take her in a sleigh across frozen Devils Lake. They were married that same day at the town of Devils Lake.

It was necessary to have duplicate marriage certificates made out since Queen Victoria had requested that one be sent to her.

The thermometer registered 40 degrees below zero when the bridal couple left Devils Lake in the "one-horse open sleigh" — the bride holding up a tiny parasol to shield her face from the biting wind. On arriving at Rolla, Marie found that her log cabin was not yet completed, and that neighbors were to accomodate her and Harry until their own home should be ready.

In the one room of their first small house, the trunks from

England were stacked against the wall. The Queen had made sure that this favored maid-in-waiting should have many reminders of the regal days she had left behind her. For Mrs. Harry Williams, farmer's wife, the trunks provided not only an elegant wardrobe to last her for many years but also many pleasant hours of displaying the contents to neighbors while relating stories concerning each item.

There was, for example, the court train, 6 yards in length and bearing still the marks of the jewels mounted upon it while Queen Victoria wore it at some state function. Gowns of heavy silk, elaborately embroidered after the fashion of the day. Nightgowns of Irish linen that once were worn by the Queen, and were initialed "V. C." Skirts from the wardrobe of Her Majesty — each with two matching waists, one with long sleeves and a high collar for cold weather, the other with elbow length sleeves and a low neck for warm weather and more formal wear.

In one trunk had been packed a complete set of sterling silverware which, years later, was used by boarders. It happened that after returning from a trip to England, Mr. and Mrs. Williams took over the management of a rooming house at Rolla — their farm having been rented for the season. Not wanting to go to the expense of purchasing flat silver for their boarders, they simply used the solid silver the Queen had given. Few of the paying guests knew the real worth of this tableware, much less did they guess that it once had graced a palace table.

There was the paperweight of Egyptian marble, exquisitely inlaid. A brooch with lapislazuli setting. A small black parasol lined with purple satin. The watch presented by the Queen as a rebuke for being tardy one time — and later set in a mantel clock case of black Russian leather with silver trimming.

From the Empress Eugenie, there was a silver loving cup, a dainty dressing gown which she herself had worn, and a manicure set. And there were jewels of many kinds. Diamonds which Marie Williams sold to relieve financial stress. Other diamonds procured additional farm land. A few of the diamonds which once had graced a tiara worn by the last Empress of France, Marie Williams sold to John Burke when he was Governor of North Dakota.

Once, viewing the trunks of castle treasure tiered against the walls of the Williams farmhouse, Mrs. Burke, the Governor's wife, asked her hostess the natural question: "Wasn't it hard to leave such an interesting position to come to live on the prairie?"

With simple sincerity, this woman who had held such a trusted place in a great monarch's service and affections, answered: "Oh, my dear, liberty is so sweet!"

14 Cowboy Doctor and Talented Daughter

A TREELESS cow town of six saloons and a few frame stores with pretentious fronts, Dickinson — in the autumn of 1883 — sprawled beside the glistening new rails of the Northern Pacific. In September its seven-hundred inhabitants had cheered President Arthur and General Sheridan as they paused briefly in the dusty village on their return from the driving of the Golden Spike.

Already the booming town boasted a weekly newspaper to chronicle local events. Items reported in the early issues picture life in the pioneer community: The Marquis de Mores had just given "an elegant Winchester rifle" to Vic Smith, local buffalo hunter. — Six hundred antelope grazed out beyond the Heart River one early October day. — A band of 500 Gros Ventres Indians from the Fort Berthold reservation came through town on their way west to hunt buffalo. — Just a few days earlier, that tribe's hereditary enemy, the Sioux, were in the vicinity, 3000 strong, and reported setting fire to

Victor H. Stickney, "The Cowboy Doctor"

the range grass in order to drive the dwindling herds of bison onto their own reservation.

And: Villard House opened with a "grand ball" at which guests were served ice cream, cakes, and oranges. — Vic Smith and Frank Chase killed a bear near Killdeer Mountain. — The Daughters of the Prairie were planning a November oyster supper. — There was editorial talk about building sidewalks.

The issue of October 6 reported: "Dr. Victor H. Stickney arrived last Saturday from Ludlow, Vermont and has located here for the practice of medicine . . . He may be found at Davis and Fowler's drugstore."

Victor Hugo Stickney, M. D., little realized on that October day that the area of his professional practice would embrace over 50,000 square miles of the old cow country — an area stretching from the Canadian border to the Black Hills; from Glendive, Montana east toward Mandan.

The young doctor immediately purchased a horse, and was shortly riding over butte-studded prairies, across coulees and breaks, and down Badlands canyons, to minister his skills.

One of his first calls came from the Joe Woods ranch more than a hundred miles north of Dickinson. Here, young Sidney Tarbell had accidentally lassoed two wild horses at once, and was jerked so violently from his mount that several of his bones were broken, a few protruding from his flesh.

Anguished by pain and weakening from loss of blood, the youth lay upon an improvised pallet while one of his friends rode at breakneck speed for "Doc" Stickney. At ranches along his way, the cowboy courier exchanged exhausted mounts for fresh ones. Relentlessly, he spurred his horse, his thought ever of the pain-twisted face and the groanings of strong Sidney Tarbell.

As he neared Dickinson, the messenger began to fear that he might not find Doc Stickney in town. The physician might well be fifty miles south, in the Wolf Butte territory . . . or west in Montana on the Pierre Wibaux ranch.

But Doc Stickney was in his Dickinson office. He lost no time securing his surgical kit to the saddle and speeding off over the trail alone, for Tarbell's friend had need to return at slower pace.

The doctor repeated the relay of horses. When he reached a spot on the Little Missouri, not far from Joe Woods' place, he found waiting for him there, a rancher with an extra horse. "Give the horse free rein," the man advised, "and he'll get you across."

The crossing made, Doc urged his fresh mount up a precipitous trail to the rim of the Badlands. He charged over the grassy hills, but when he reached the Joe Woods ranch, there was no longer any need for a surgeon.

Already the cowboy's friends had digged Sidney Tarbell a grave. Now they stood about Doc Stickney, sober-faced, expectantly. Silently the bronzed men implored him to do one last ministration for Sidney Tarbell. And the prairie doctor read Scripture beside the broken body and offered up a prayer. Then he turned from what was the first white man's grave in McKenzie County, and began the long ride back to Dickinson.

Such grueling rides became commonplace. Many times the destination was a cowboys' camp, and weary though he might be on arrival, Doc must operate for a gunshot wound, or set a splintered bone. Sometimes he operated out under the sun, with an inverted mess wagon box as the table. There were no white-clad, skilled assistants to help him. Only bronzed cowhands or homesteaders — sometimes silent Indians — stood waiting, helpless. He must sterilize the instruments himself — in a Dutch oven; he must give the anesthetic.

During the first two years that the "Cowboy Doctor" — as he came to be called — traversed the lonely miles, his thoughts were often of the pretty little dressmaker waiting for him back at Ludlow — sweet Maggie Hayes sewing in her spare hours on a wedding dress of cream brocaded satin trimmed with lace.

And so Victor Stickney bought a house on the corner of Sims and Oak, and converted one of its rooms into an office. On September 12, 1885 he was at Bismarck to meet his bride. "We'll have to be married here, Maggie," he told her, "This is the only place out this way where there is a priest. — The train will wait only 20 minutes."

There was not enough time to change into the cherished wedding gown; Margaret Effie Hayes wore her dusty traveling dress as she spoke her vows with Victor Hugo Stickney.

More surprises awaited the bride in the new home to which her doctor husband brought her. She was frightened at first when Indians peered at her through the windows of the house at Sims and Oak. She soon learned, however, to proceed with her cooking and baking while Indians, waiting for hot doughnuts, squatted about the floor of her kitchen.

Maggie learned to hold the lamp close while Doc performed surgery in the little office room. But, the operation concluded, she would excuse herself and sometimes go out on the dark porch to faint in private.

One day on a Dickinson street, the Cowboy Doctor met a man who limped and who seemed "all teeth and eyes." The stranger inquired of him, "Could you tell me where I can find the doctor?"

"Indeed," smiled Stickney, "I am the doctor."

"My name is Roosevelt," said the stranger, "Theodore Roosevelt — deputy sheriff. I just put two men in jail. Now my feet need some attention."

While the doctor attended him, the spectacled deputy sheriff glowed with boyish satisfaction as he related how he had caught the two men after they had stolen a boat — a crime then considered almost as despicable as stealing a man's horse. It had taken two days to get the men to the jail, and rough travel it had been — the ordeal included the fording of streams filled with floating ice. No wink of sleep had the sheriff dared to take since the time of the capture.

When Roosevelt had gone, Victor Stickney enthusiastically reported to Maggie, "I've just met the most peculiar, and at the same time, the most wonderful man I've ever come to know."

Out on his long errands by horse, or buckboard, Doc was frequently hungry and in need of rest when he was miles from home. But the hospitality of the prairie people knew no bounds when the respected and familiar figure approached. The greetings at ranch home, settler's shanty, or cowboys' camp were usually of brusque good will:

"Wall, hello, Pills! Turn your horse loose in the corral, and come on in and get next to the beans!"

"Light, Doc! Be neighborly! The sirloin's a-broilin' an' it'll be a joy to see ya carvin' somethin' that don't hurt!"

But there were many times when weariness overcame him miles from any chimney fire, and then he could only wrap himself in a tarpaulin and sleep on the prairie's bosom.

When blizzards lashed across the plains, he would seek shelter in a brush patch, or in the lee of a butte or huge boulder. If homeward bound in his sleigh when a blinding snowstorm caught him, he would give his horses a clip with the whip, loose the reins, and let them find their way home.

The Cowboy Doctor learned to love the buffalo-grass country and the hardy western folks. But the center of his life was the home at Sims and Oak. Always Maggie waited for him with her "thousand welcomes," and, in time, the two little daughters, Marjorie and Dorothy, were there to draw his heart.

When Dorothy was not yet a year old, her vision seemed impaired. The anxious parents took her to a St. Paul hospital where specialists performed the first of seven corneal ulcer operations. Doc Stickney left his afflicted baby and his wife at St. Paul, and returned to his patients. During the lonely months that followed, he found time to pull cottonwood saplings from the Heart River banks to plant around the house and to transplant woodbine to make shade for the porch. Then one joyful day in June, Maggie and little Dorothy were once again home.

Marjorie was delighted with a baby sister who wore dark

glasses. For the baby, Maggie made sun bonnets lined with dark green, and wheeled her about in a carriage. Neighbors inquired solicitously, "Is the baby blind?" and Mrs. Stickney would reply, indignantly, "Of course, she isn't."

But until Dorothy was eighteen years old, there were to be intermittent periods when she must sit in a room with shades tightly drawn, wearing bandages over her eyes. So Doc Stickney read to his little daughter, read Dickens and Stevenson, Mark Twain and Eugene Fields. In those golden times of sharing the world's great literature, a special bond grew between Dorothy and her father.

Doc Stickney got his little girls buffalo-calf coats for the cold winters. He provided them with small Indian ponies of their own. Once when they were away with relatives, during a Dickinson smallpox epidemic, he built a playhouse for them. One winter he flooded the backyard to make a skating rink for them and their friends.

Mother Stickney regularly planted sweet peas, nasturtiums and poppies against the corral fence. Summers, when scorching wind, grasshoppers or hail assailed her flowers, she would stand in the bay window and look out upon the ravaged garden. "I'll never plant another garden," she would sob. But when spring came again, she would plant anew.

During World War I, Doc Stickney was commissioned a lieutenant, later a captain, in the Army Medical Corps; but he was disappointed in not being called for overseas duty. He had not long returned to civilian practice when grief filled his heart; a fatal illness had laid hold upon his Maggie. That last summer she was with him, she often lay in a bed on the woodbine-shaded porch, and Victor Stickney would bring her goldenrod and other flowers from the prairie.

On December 24, 1921, Maggie slipped away from him, and the house at Sims and Oak became a lonely place. Marjorie had married young Dr. A. P. Nachtwey. Dorothy, her eyesight regained, was in New York, trying to break into the theatre. Frequently now, the Cowboy Doctor went East to visit her.

In the early months of 1927, Doc, himself, became ill. The diagnosis was "inoperable cancer." He knew that only a few months remained, and, giving his friends no hint of what awaited him — he quietly put his affairs in order.

From Dorothy came a joyous letter inviting him East for a June wedding — she was marrying Howard Lindsay, a man Doc had met and liked immensely. But scarcely had Dorothy mailed this letter when she received from Marjorie the news that caused her to quit the play in which she was acting, and speed home to her dying father.

To the last — which was in July of 1927 — the Cowboy Doctor kept in cheerful spirits. He did not discuss his condition, but talked excitedly with Dorothy about young Charles Lindbergh who had just flown non-stop across the Atlantic.

Stickney Hall stands today on the campus of the Dickinson State Teachers College which Doc Stickney first helped to establish. But the greatest memorial to the Cowboy Doctor is the love which is enshrined in the hearts of the prairie people who knew the healing in his hands.

Doc Stickney would have exulted in the fame which was to come to the daughter whose dark days he had shared with such tenderness and compassion, the girl to whom he imparted his own courage and determination. After seventeen years of recurring blindness, Dorothy Stickney was healed, and she was able to enter upon a career in the theatre.

Her first five years were disheartening. Either she could find no work, or else she played in third-rate vaudeville acts or road companies. For seven summers she played stock at Skowhegan, Maine.

There it was that a producer saw her acting and signed her for a promising part in "The Nervous Wreck," a road company play. But when Dorothy returned to New York, the playwright dismissed her on sight — she was "not the type."

She left the playwright's office in tearful despair — and met a young man named Howard Lindsay who gave her some advice about "behaving well in a bad situation." A year later, he was at Skowhegan to direct the same stock company in which Dorothy was playing.

That same summer, Dorothy chanced to read the manuscript of a new play, "Chicago." One of the characters was "Crazy Liz" — a dirty, middle-aged, ugly hag in jail for murder. Young, blue-eyed, blond Dorothy was convinced that this was just the part for her.

Of this she was unable to convince the play agent, the author, or the associate producer. Not even after she came to them in "Crazy Liz" costume — a slovenly black dress, a hideous black hat, her hair straggled back, her face lined and shadowed. But she did wangle a promise that she would be allowed to try out for the part once the play was in rehearsal.

Dorothy was playing the part of a sweet little ingénue in "The Squall" when she heard that "Chicago" was preparing for rehearsal. Immediately, she put on her hag make-up and rushed over to the office of Sam Harris, the producer, and reminded him of the promise to let her try out.

"Don't be silly," Harris replied, "you're in a hit play, now. Stay there. Anyway, we have an actress engaged for this 'Crazy Liz' part."

Then the determined Dorothy asked — and was granted — permission to watch the first rehearsal. When the actress signed for "Crazy Liz" failed to appear, Dorothy was asked if she would like to try out.

She had not seen the play manuscript for six months. Now she was given only a few minutes to scan the copy before she was called onto the stage. She gave a performance of "Crazy Liz," complete with screams. As soon as the first scene was done, Harris signed Dorothy Stickney for a three-year contract.

"Chicago" was Dorothy's first major success. She was lauded as giving "the best supporting performance of the season." When Howard Lindsay's friends would ask him about the girl he was going to marry, he delighted telling them, "She's playing 'Crazy Liz' in 'Chicago'," and then watching

Miss Dorothy Stickney

Miss Stickney as "Crazy Liz"

their startled reactions as they recalled the screaming, horrid-looking hag.

It was while rejoicing in this early success that Dorothy received the news of her father's fatal illness and went home.

After "Chicago," there was no lack for good parts. But ill health dogged Miss Stickney, and there were times when she feared she must give up her work. Then her husband and Russel Crouse began work on a play called "Life With Father." Dorothy and Howard Lindsay borrowed money so that he could work on the play — when both could have taken lucrative jobs doing pictures in Hollywood.

Their faith in the play was vindicated when "Life With Father" was produced on Broadway — with Dorothy and her husband playing the father and mother. But they little dreamed that the play would break the world's record for the longest run; it played for almost eight years in New York. Dorothy and Howard were in the play for five years.

"Life With Mother" followed, and other Broadway productions such as "The Small Hours," "To Be Continued," and "Kind Sir." And there have been parts for Dorothy in nearly a dozen films.

Her outstanding ability as an actress has been widely acclaimed. For her portrayal of "Vinnie" in "Life With Father," Dorothy was given the Barter Award. Bowdoin College, in 1951, awarded her an honorary degree.

In May 1954, she came back to Dickinson as an honor guest.

In the old home town she visited with friends who had known her those years when she sometimes had to live for weeks at a time in a darkened room in the house on Sims and Oak. And many Dickinson folks reminisced about the Cowboy Doctor for they beheld in his talented daughter the same friendly and valiant spirit that had endeared Doc Stickney to the people of the butte-studded prairies.

15 Liver-Eating Johnson

DOUBTLESS the most blood-thirsty character to inhabit the Little Missouri area during Territorial days was "Liver-Eating" Johnson, a giant of a fellow with black-whiskered face.

Once, with a company of hunters, he went westward into Montana and one morning came upon a war-party of encamped Sioux. One of the white men, venturing too near the hostile Indians, was killed by an arrow.

Shortly after this happened, a heavy rain fell, rendering the Indians' bows and arrows all but useless since the bow strings were soaked. The white men, with their guns, opened fire and routed the Indians.

Johnson, in company with a squaw-man, Henry Keiser, surprised a brave and a youth of about fifteeen in a copse of trees. At the sight of the white pursuers, the two Indians began to run.

"You take the boy — I'll get that brave," Johnson said to Keiser. In only seconds the great-limbed Johnson had captured and felled the retreating warrior.

While the Indian was yet alive, this savage white man slashed his victim's belly, ripped out the liver and started gorging.

As Johnson's whiskers filled with warm blood, he remarked to his companion, "It's good — better than antelope liver."

16 "Gunnysack Bill"

OUT in the ranch lands of southwestern North Dakota there once roamed an hombre known as "Gunnysack Bill.' What his real name was, nobody but "Gunny" himself knew.

Other cowpokes observed that Gunnysack was careful never to cross the Montana border; they discovered that the sheriff at Wibaux had a warrant out for Gunny's arrest, the charge being horse-stealing. For reasons that he managed to keep to himself, Gunnysack never made excursions to the South, either, though he was heard to hanker for Texas, the state of his birth.

And Gunnysack did abominate the North Dakota winters. His toes were always tortured by the cold. So he tied gunnysacks around his boots, even wrapped the sacks about his saddle stirrups.

Because of this habit, the cowpunchers dubbed him "Gunnysack Bill." The moniker served to distinguish him from the other local Bills — Turkey Track Bill, Molash Bill, Curlee Bill, Texas Bill and several plain Bills.

Gunnysack occasionally went to town to celebrate. After inbibing considerable liquor, he usually got into a bloody scrape with other rugged celebrants. Sometimes he came out of these wrangles with bloody gashes. But Gunnysack never thought of bothering Doc Stickney; he "healed" his wounds by searing them with a hot branding iron.

17 "Mustache Maud"

MUSTACHE Maud had legitimate right to her nickname and it fitted well a woman of her robustness and mannish ways. While not totally lacking in femininity, she toted a pistol, and was known to have taking ways with cattle and a special knack for rustling hogs.

Her apparel was a large-brimmed sombrero, cowboy boots and short skirts — this in the Gay Nineties, when a proper lady's dress trailed upon the ground. From the pocket of her shirt there always dangled the tag of a tobacco pouch — Mustache Maud rolled her own.

With her Texas cowpoke husband, Ott Black, she drifted into Winona, situated on the east bank of the Missouri across from Fort Yates. A roistering cluster of six saloons, two dance halls, two stores, a makeshift hotel and a post office — this was Winona in its first years. The inhabitants of the tawdry town were mostly gamblers, saloonkeepers, bartenders and dance hall girls; and soldiers from the Fort Yates military post and cowpunchers of the area came there for drunken revelry. Mustache Maud and her husband added a saloon and gambling den to Winona's business section.

Mingling freely with the quick-shooting customers, Mustache Maud, a six-shooter holstered at her hip, held her own. Gunshots enlivened the ribald nights at Winona. Sordid incidents were not uncommon and there were tragedies.

"Mustache Maud" Black   Frank B. Fiske

When the Spicer family north of town was murdered by Indians crazed with fire-water, Winona residents quickly lynched the murderers. A variety-show girl committed suicide, died on the dance-hall floor.

As a stable citizenry settled in the area, Winona's ill-famed business ceased to flourish. Mustache Maud and Ott moved out, went to a place called Seim at the forks of the Grand River in western South Dakota. Here they procured an old log building, tossed some more dirt upon the sod roof, and built a ship-lap bar.

Later, the pair engaged in ranching in the Badlands area west of Fort Yates. Mustache Maud was the executive type; she managed the business for over a decade. She frequently took charge of crews of men — whether the work was making hay or branding calves.

On one occasion she arrived at a hay camp by dawn and found her men still asleep in their bed rolls. As the foreman lifted his drowsy head at the intrusion, she surveyed him with a dangerous eye. "See here," she drawled in her deep voice, "we ain't got no cures for bed sores around here."

Once when Frank Zahn and Frank Fiske called at her ranch, they noticed several rattlesnakes coiled about in her yard. "Don't be afraid of them snakes," Mustache Maud advised, "they ain't no worse than some people I know." Then she went out and killed some chickens and served her guests tasty stew with dumplings.

Under her brusque exterior, there beat a tender and kind heart. If a neighbor's child lacked clothing, Mustache Maud managed somehow to procure what was needed. When a neighbor's wife lay ill, or a man was short of feed for his stock, none was more quick to come with assistance than this gun-toting woman.

When the Blacks were in the cattle business, neighboring ranchers observed that their herd made mysterious increases. Mustache Maud was brought to court at Fort Yates to answer charges of cattle stealing. When she made her appearance her masculine garb excited great attention. On the witness stand, she showed amazing composure and always succeeded in baffling the attorneys.

Once, when an exceptionally large crowd had gathered in the Fort Yates courtroom to appraise this strange woman of the old, wild West, Mustache Maud surprised them all. She came attired in a dress of demure blue linen, and as she sat in the witness stand during the cross-examination, she crocheted lace.

18 *Flying Cloud*

A BLACK cowhide now upholstering a chair in the home of Judge Frank B. Zahn at Fort Yates once served as circumstantial evidence that Mustache Maud had taking ways with cattle.

That unusual chair is only one of many fascinating museum pieces to be viewed at the Zahn home. Here the visitor may handle Sitting Bull's scalping knife and the whetstone the famous medicine man used for sharpening it. Besides an array of Sioux Indian clothes, headdresses, finery and weapons, Zahn has historic possessions such as the silver peace medal given to Chief Cottonwood by Lewis and Clark in 1803, the peace medal presented to Chief Crazy Horse by Indian commissioners at Fort Laramie, the brass crucifix that Father De Smet gave to Chief White Bull, and a peace pipe once owned by Chief Fire Heart. Among some personal treasures to be seen here are appreciation awards to Judge Zahn from three Presidents — Calvin Coolidge, Franklin Roosevelt and Harry Truman.

Judge Zahn's museum is not just a collection. It is the heritage of an extraordinary career.

Flying Cloud
(Judge Frank B. Zahn)

His father, William P. Zahn, served as a soldier under General George Custer, being discharged August 22, 1875. For three years, he then drove bull-teams, freighting between Bismarck and Deadwood. Next he established an Indian trading post on the Cannon Ball River, and there married a sister of Chief John Grass. Following the death of this wife, he married Kize-win, daughter of the Sioux Chief Flying Cloud. Later, he traveled with Buffalo Bill's Wild West Show as interpreter. He was a personal friend of Jim Bridger, Calamity Jane, Father De Smet and famous Indians such as Sitting Bull, Rain-in-the-Face, Gall, Spotted Tail, and Red Cloud.

Frank Zahn was born in a tepee on May 4, 1890 at the Chief Redfish camp near the Cannon Ball River. From his father, he learned the English language; and from his Indian mother, the Sioux tongue. He was given the Indian name of "Flying Cloud." After graduating from Carlisle Indian University, he served in World War I, then for two years attended Aaker's Business College at Fargo.

Returning to Fort Yates, he began his long service as interpreter. During 26 years of such work, he did translating for notables among both Indians and white men: White Bull, One Bull, Red Tomahawk, General H. L. Scott, President Herbert Hoover, Vice President Charles Curtis and Queen Marie of Rumania.

He served for a time on the Tribal Council of the Standing Rock Agency. Then in 1940, with fifteen descendents of Sitting Bull, he went to Hollywood where he played the leading Indian chief in "They Died With Their Boots On." Following this he worked in two other Western films, "Wild Bill Hickock Rides" and "Sioux City."

Home again at Fort Yates, he was appointed Senior Judge of the Standing Rock Indian Jurisdiction, the position he now holds.

19 Red Tomahawk

IN the cold winter dawn of December 15, 1890, three Indian policemen pushed open the door of Sitting Bull's cabin on the Grand River in South Dakota.

"We have come to arrest you," Lieutenant Bull Head informed the medicine man.

Sitting Bull offered no resistance. Since his surrender to life as a Reservation ward, the old Sioux leader had steadfastly championed whatever he believed to be the best interests of his people — but had carefully avoided antagonizing Agency authorities by any act of violence or open opposition. Now he quietly dressed, and made ready to go with the police.

Lieutenant Bull Head took one arm of the medicine man, Shave Head the other. Red Tomahawk, the third policeman, followed behind.

Outside the cabin, the three policemen and their captive faced a quickly-gathering and sullen group of Sitting Bull's "Ghost Dancers." Among them stood Crow Foot, the medicine man's own son.

The youth surveyed his father with scorn. "You call yourself a brave man? You vowed you would never surrender to a blue-coat! Now you give yourself into the hands of these men with metal breasts!"

The words seared the soul of proud old Sitting Bull. Glancing desperately about him, he could see that the police force of some forty men was easily outnumbered. Seeing the faces of so many loyal followers about him, he suddenly screeched out the order to attack.

Shots splintered the air.

Shave Head fell, riddled by bullets. Lieutenant Bull Head tottered to the ground — but, shooting as he fell, wounded

Red Tomahawk

Frank B. Fiske photo

Frank B. Fiske

Sitting Bull in the side. From behind, Red Tomahawk fired the shot that killed the medicine man.

Then quickly, Red Tomahawk took charge, and ordered the "blue-coats" into Sitting Bull's cabin for safety. Behind them, four of their number lay dead.

Enraged over the slaying of Sitting Bull, of his son Crow Foot and several braves, the 160 hostiles scurried into nearby thickets and from this ambush began pouring fire upon the cabin.

No return shots spat from the cabin for the Indian policemen were almost out of ammunition.

Then over the hill, a mile to the north, came the Eighth Cavalry, under the command of Captain E. G. Fechet.

At sight of the Cavalry, the hostiles mounted and fled.

Red Tomahawk and his men raised a white flag as the soldiers rapidly approached the camp. When the cavalry arrived, they buried the slain braves, then loaded the bodies of the policemen and of the medicine man into a wagon and brought them to Fort Yates for burial.

Sitting Bull had led his last uprising — his life ended by a bullet fired by the young Sioux, Red Tomahawk.

Born the "Winter when Wolf Robe was Killed by the Pawnees," Red Tomahawk was raised in the lodges of his people, and early trained as a warrior. At the age of sixteen, he was among the braves who harrassed the military post at Fort Rice. After engaging in seven battles for his tribe, he was called Red Tomahawk — an honored name which had been handed down for seven generations.

Standing 6 feet 4 inches in his mocassins, Red Tomahawk was a superb physical specimen when he was in his prime. He was straight as an arrow and as lithe as a bow string.

Respected by white men, a champion of his own people, Marcellus Red Tomahawk was not an hereditary chief but attained a chieftain's status. Twice he went to Washington to plead the cause of his Sioux brothers. He sat in council with three presidents: U. S. Grant, Theodore Roosevelt, and Herbert Hoover. While Marshal Foch, of France, was on a visit to this country, Red Tomahawk smoked the peace pipe with the renowned World War I leader and adopted him into the Sioux tribe.

After serving for nearly ten years on the Indian police force at Standing Rock Reservation, Red Tomahawk resigned in 1895 to become assistant "boss farmer" on the Agency demonstration farm at Cannon Ball. This position he retained until a few years before his death at the age of 82, on August 7, 1931.

It is Red Tomahawk's profile that we see on state highway markers in North Dakota. This honor came to the Indian leader in 1923 when the State Highway Commission designed the official road marker.

20 *Brother to the Sioux*

LATE in the afternoon of April 15, 1889 the George Fiske family arrived, by wagon, in Mustache Maud's metropolis of Winona. From this town they could see Fort Yates, their destination, across the Missouri.

They were rowed across the tawny river, and soon reached the military post situated on the mile-long plateau. Shortly, five-year-old Frank Bennett Fiske was happily at home with the Sioux, a people with whom he would live the most of his life, and a people whose history he would preserve through photography and the written word.

About a year and a half later, Frank was standing in front of the Agency store when a long-to-be-remembered incident occurred. A wagon procession escorted by cavalrymen and Indian policemen entered the village, and quickly a crowd of Sioux gathered about — for in one of the wagons rested the body of the famed Sioux medicine man, Sitting Bull.

Frank and his playmates watched as the corpse was carried into the "dead house." They were still watching when, toward dusk, the canvas-wrapped body, in a pine board coffin, was brought out and placed in a wagon and taken to the military cemetery for burial.

Frank's father served as wagonmaster at Fort Yates, so the young boy first attended a school for Post employees' children. Later, he studied at the Government boarding school.

As a lad, Frank herded cows for Fort families, driving his charges out to graze upon the surrounding hills. To earn a little spending money, he would gather up beer bottles and take them to Winona where he sold them to Mustache Maud and other saloonkeepers there. As he grew older, he worked as a cabin boy on Missouri River steamers, and helped at Ed Fansler's photograph studio.

When — in October, 1900 — Fansler failed to return from the South to resume his business, Frank obtained permission from the commanding officer to open a studio of his own. Thus was begun a picture-making career which eventually was to produce hundreds of Indian photographs — the most outstanding Sioux collection now existing.

While Frank was getting established in the photograph shop, a young lady, Miss Angela Cournoyer, came to Fort Yates to visit a sister. Angela was the great-granddaughter of Forked Horn, the Yanktonaii Sioux chief. Angela and Frank were immediately attracted to one another, but marriage was something that neither could consider for some time. Feeling the need for additional training, Frank went to Bismarck to work in the Butler studio; Angela returned to South Dakota where she entered the University to study piano and voice.

The following spring, Frank was back at Fort Yates. Fascinating though he found the Indian photography to be, it was not sufficiently lucrative. So he worked as an assistant pilot on river steamers operated then by I. P. Baker of Bismarck. For the next five spring and fall seasons (when river shipping was at its maximum), he assisted such men as the famous Captain Grant Marsh, in operating river freighters.

Between river trips, he would be working at his Fort Yates studio and using spare time on a book *The Taming of the Sioux* which was published in 1917. Then, with America at war, Frank boarded the *Scarab* down river to St. Louis where he enlisted in the Army.

Released from Army service, he came home by way of Armour, South Dakota where lived the "girl he left behind him." Angela and Frank were married on his birthday, June 11, 1919, and came to Fort Yates to live.

The photgraphy business was still more pleasurable than profitable, so Angela taught at the Agency school, and Frank became county auditor. He served in this position for three years, then exchanged positions with J. R. Harmon, the county treasurer.

It was in 1923 that Angela wrote a three-act play "The Cry of Lone Eagle" which won the Vold Prize awarded by the University of North Dakota. Encouraged by their friends, Angela and Frank decided to produce the play. After organizing a troupe of seventeen players, they showed the play in a number of North Dakota cities and, in 1937, brought it to a national folk festival in Chicago.

For ten years Fiske edited and published the Fort Yates *Pioneer Arrow*. In 1933, he published his *Life and Death of Sitting Bull*.

Always, Fiske was intensely interested in Sioux legend and history. While editing the Fort Yates newspaper, he began collecting information for a history of the Standing Rock Reservation.

To help gather material for this book, he undertook a rather unusual canoe journey. In 1947, accompanied by William Lemons, a Fort Yates English teacher, he went to Hardin, Montana near the site of the Battle of the Little Big Horn, and there, at the confluence of the Big Horn and Little Horn rivers, embarked in a 14-foot canoe *Far West II* and began a 750-mile trip down river.

Through Hell-Roarin' Rapids, past the jutting cliffs and swirling eddies of the Yellowstone, the sandbars and whirlpools of the Missouri, Fiske and Lemons made their precarious way. At dusk, they would select a likely spot and set up their tent. Along the way, Frank visited with old-timers he had known as a young river pilot and exchanged yarns about early river characters.

The weather was ideal until the two reached Washburn where a rainstorm whipped the Old Muddy into fury, and caused the voyageurs a four-day delay. On June 22 when they reached Bismarck, they were too late to join in that city's Diamond Jubilee Celebration.

But altogether, the canoe journey was for 64-year-old Frank Fiske a delightful and sentimental experience, and rewarding in the matter of additional material for his cherished Sioux history book.

In 1950 a heart attack confined him to the Veterans' Hospital at Fargo, but by that time most of the book had been written. At this time, he was notified of a signal honor: the presentation, by the American Artists Professional League, of the North Dakota art award in recognition of his outstanding Indian portraits.

The labor of love that had culminated in this award was one extending over forty years. Early in his efforts to procure the sittings of austere and often suspicious and superstitious chiefs, Frank Fiske had become adept at persuasion. Often this persuasion took the form of a shining silver dollar.

Among those persuaded to pose by the grace of the silver dollar was Red Tomahawk. After several silver dollars, Fiske obtained a number of excellent portraits of this noted Sioux. It was at the request of the State Highway Commission that Fiske made the photograph of Red Tomahawk from which came the profile now used on state highway markers.

Other famous Indians that sat for Fiske were Rain-in-the-Face, John Grass, White Bull, One Bull, and Mary Crawler — the girl who took part in the charge against Major Reno in the Battle of the Little Big Horn. Fiske also photographed a number of memorable white men of Teritorial days; these included Major James McLaughlin, Alex McKenzie, Captain Belk, and General Hugh Scott.

With his devoted wife's help, Frank Bennett Fiske in 1951 completed the manuscript of *History of the Standing Rock Indian Reservation*. But on July 18, 1952, the manuscript still unpublished, this memorable photographer and historian died at a Bismarck hospital at the age of 69.

21 Fiddler, Regardless

TED Anderson, when ten years old, lost his right arm in an accident. But that did not cause him to cast aside his fiddle, the delight of his life. The boy decided that, somehow, he would again make his fiddle sing for him.

He tried sticking the bow firmly under the short stub of right arm and, with the left hand, fingering and moving the upside-down instrument back and forth on top of the steadied bow. After months of effort he was able to produce only some off-pitch squawks and screeches.

But it was not in Ted Anderson to give up. Gradually, as the months became years, he gained control. The squawks and screeches gave way to sounds that were music.

He took along the fiddle when, in 1904, as a grown man he went to drive freight for the Milwaukee Railway Company. Despite his handicap he managed to handle a 6-horse wagon as well as any of the men hauling grain and supplies for the railway construction crew.

When the freighters camped for the night, Ted and his pal, "Rusty" Holman, competed at the job of peeling the supper potatoes. Ted would stick a fork in his potato, thrust the fork handle where his fiddle bow belonged, and proceed to peel. He beat Rusty every time.

The supper eaten, Ted would get his fiddle, Rusty his guitar, and the two would fill the prairie quiet with cowboy songs.

Ted later worked as a cowboy on ranches in southwestern

North Dakota. The boy whose determination had earned him the joy of his own music-making became the man who not only could manage a freighter wagon as well as the best mule-skinner — but one who also could pitch hay, lasso, or shoe horses as efficiently as any ranch hand.

At Bowman, in 1920, Ted Anderson met and married Ruby Love. They lived for a time at Amidon where Ted served as register of deeds. They next went to the Marmarth area where Ted managed a ranch.

Once, for a short time, he was a paid violinist. The Jack Guth Show came along, boasting the world's biggest steer, one weighing 3900 pounds. The show manager saw in Ted Anderson another kind of boast. So, for the season, Ted was featured as the: "One-Armed Violinist."

When World War II started, Anderson took his wife and children to Salem, Oregon where he worked as a welder in a defense plant.

Death claimed Ted Anderson not long after, and the world lost a kind and contented spirit. Often, Ted had declared: "I have everything in life that a man with two arms could have."

22 *Badlands Artist*

THE grass in the sheltered draws withered, dried as had the bunch grass on the hills and plateaus. Springs that once spilled into coulees and nurtured marsh grass, dwindled to mere trickles; some ceased altogether.

As the springs diminished, so did the herds of white-faced cattle. Heifers and cows too gaunt to survive a winter, were driven from the brown seared hills and shipped to market. Here and there on the prairie hills, and in the shelter of Badlands coverts, lay the deep-ribbed carcasses of cattle whose bellies no longer gnawed from hunger.

Discouraged and bankrupt, many North Dakota farmers and ranchers sold their goods at auction. They boarded shut the windows of homes that had known family laughter and visitings with neighbors. They left the empty house to the soughing of wind and sifting of dust through widening cracks.

But there were more who stayed; the plague of drouth could not ravage their stubborn faith in the prairie land.

One of these was Einar Olstad, a Sentinel Butte rancher. With most of his cattle gone, he discovered that he had something that he had not had for many years — periods of leisure.

One fall day in 1935, he knew what to do with that spare time, for a package came that day from his sister Olga and his niece, Beatrice Bragstad. They sent him a box of brushes and an assortment of oil paints. An accompanying message said: "You always enjoyed painting when you were a boy. Why don't you try it again?"

Einar Olstad *would* "try it again." He had burned his first brushes, had tried to forget his great delight in painting; he was twenty when his father died, and left him the responsibility of supporting his mother and six children. And so, for the next two decades, Einar had worked at forge and anvil in the father's blacksmith shop at Sioux Falls, South Dakota; there had been no time to paint, no need for brushes and oil tubes.

In 1919, he and his wife and young son went to Marmath, North Dakota and there he engaged in ranching. Some years later, he moved to his present ranch 17 miles southeast of Sentinel Butte.

With his new box of paints, Einar settled himself in a well-lighted room of his ranchhouse, and sought to recapture his boyhood delight in painting. Soon he was telling his neighbors, "You forget your troubles when you paint — there's something about working with colors that takes you right out of yourself."

He painted the scenes about him — the buttes, the bunchgrass acres, the white-faced cattle, the cowboys. He produced paintings having the vitality of the cattle country which has been home to Einar almost half a century.

He portrayed the grimness of the drouth that had desolated the land, in such stark scenes as "Badlands Bull" and "Drought of '36" — the latter depicting a starving young calf beside its dead mother. One of these paintings was later accepted by the National Exhibition of American Art in New York City.

But few of Olstad's canvasses are of grim subjects. The humor that is a dominant trait in the artist's nature is observed in numbers of his scenes. Many of these portray actual anecdotes.

"In "The Banker and the Rancher," we see a mounted cattle man and a distressfully saddle-sore man of finance still astride a horse. The cattle man wants a loan. The banker wants to see the cattle that must be security for the loan. The rancher has taken the banker on what has become — for the man accustomed to sitting in a swivel chair — an insufferably long ride. And the rancher is ever pointing to the distant hills, and saying: "The cattle are over there." The banker, eventually, grants the loan without inspecting the security.

"Forty Miles from Home" is a self-portrait. Olstad is in a dilemma. Far out on the range, his horse has bucked him off — and all the way home, that ornery beast keeps itself just out of reach of the lariat.

This rancher-artist once saw "Calamity Joe" Meyers at a funeral; and on reaching home again, painted the colorful Badlands figure from memory. He observed neighbor women chatting over their afternoon coffee, and "Kaffe Lag" resulted. "The Last Roundup" is a jolly portrayal of a Medora barber shop quartette whose counterparts in the flesh are Rusty MacMillan, Bill McCarty, John Hanson, and Bill Lawson.

Encouraged by his enthusiastic family and friends, Olstad in 1939 — at the age of 61 — decided to attend an art school. He chose the Layton School of Art in Milwaukee. Arrived there, he found all the other students to be young collegians, and was sure they would regard him as an old codger. Yet they forthrightly accepted him, and found his quality of joy

Einar Olstad at work forging iron letters for entrance signs at gates of Theodore Roosevelt National Park

Photo by courtesy of Chester L. Brooks, Park Historian

Photo showing "Rough Rider" plaque by Olstad at east entrance of Roosevelt Park

Photo by courtesy of Chester L. Brooks

"Water Hole"

"Drought of '36"

r painting by Olstad at Trinity
eran Church, Sentinel Butte

 by courtesy of the Reverend
. Olsrud, Beach

Einar Olstad standing beside his "The Good Shepherd" now hanging in the Sentinel Butte Congregational Church

in brush and palette infectious.

The artist, John Stewart Curry — there at the School — gave Olstad warm encouragement. The two months passed rapidly. The frank criticism of fellow students and the guidance of his instructors were tonic to the Sentinel Butte rancher. Spring came, and with it the need to return to the ranch — where his son Harmon was in charge. Again, though — in 1947 — Einar returned to Milwaukee for another helpful term at the School.

When Theodore Roosevelt National Park was established, Einar Olstad was the one commissioned to create suitable decorations for its native stone gate entrances. For this assignment, he went back to his anvil. The iron plaque he hammered out showed the Rough-Rider President on a bucking bronc.

Slope area residents pressed their Badlands artist for an exhibit of his work at the Park dedication, June 4, 1949. Approximately 2000 people visited the Congregational Church at Medora to see twenty-one of Olstad's western canvasses and a dozen of his painted plates.

In addition to portraying the beauty of the Badlands and the life of its people, Einar Olstad has painted murals and altar paintings for several churches in the Slope region. The wrought-iron fence which surrounds the statue of the Marquis de Mores at Medora is the handiwork of this modest man who in 1951 won national recognition when the American Artists Professional League gave him its Honor Roll Award.

23 *Rising Bear, Schoolteacher*

TO be given a second name, a name of veneration, was a distinct honor among the Hidatsa tribe of Indians. In re-naming an individual, the tribe would choose for the one being honored the name of some great warrior chief of the past. For Charles Ward Hoffman, pioneer schoolteacher of white and Arikara blood, the Hidatsa people chose the name of one of their most venerated chiefs, Rising Bear.

Born at Like-a-Fish-Hook Village in 1868, the son of a white trader father and a French-Indian and Scotch mother, he was given the name of Ni-ku-ta-wi-ksu-ta-ka (White Hawk) by Arikara relatives.

When White Hawk was still an infant, the father, Charles Wheeler Hoffman, was obliged to go East to replenish his trading store supplies, and the child's Indian relatives lost no time in kidnaping both him and his mother.

In due time, Hoffman returned, would have landed from the river steamer, but his wife's people threatened his life if he came ashore. Moreover, they declared that his baby son had died and that his wife had deserted him.

The distraught young father continued up the river to begin a new life in Montana. There, eventually, he became a leading citizen and served for eighteen years as a member of the Montana legislature.

White Hawk's mother never ceased her grieving or her watching for the husband's return. Broken-hearted, she died at an early age.

Long afterward when the son had grown to manhood and had a family of his own, the elder Hoffman learned quite by chance that his White Hawk was living and located on the Fort Berthold Indian Reservation. Quickly, he came to find him. For the remaining years of the father's life, the two kept in close touch with one another.

As a boy of seven, White Hawk earned his first money — fifty cents a week — at old Fort Berthold, by leading the missionary's cow to water. Most of the three-fourths of a mile from the Reverend C. L. Hall's barn to the shore of the Missouri, White Hawk was exposed to Hidatsa boys who stoned the cow and "accidentally" the Arikara herdsboy.

(Although the three tribes of Mandan, Hidatsa and Arikara had banded together for mutual protection against the Sioux, each tribe maintained its own section of Like-a-Fish-Hook village, each spoke its own language, and its members did not mingle socially with those of other tribes. White Hawk was therefore considered a legitimate target by the Hidatsa boys.)

He therefore forfeited his job, and did not have another regular one until he was sixteen. Then he received five dollars a month caring for a team of stage horses.

An exciting event of White Hawk's boyhood happened on a warm September afternoon in 1881. From the bank of the Missouri he spied a strange-looking man-creature come floating down the swirling waters of the wide stream. He watched it suddenly gain an upright sitting position, then heard it blow a brisk bugle salute.

Excited Indians and soldiers from nearby Fort Berthold rushed to the shore. Then the bugle-blowing visitant calmly paddled himself ashore.

White Hawk watched in amazement — the visitor was a white man wearing an inflated rubber suit; he towed a tin-and-canvas boat which held his effects: the bugle, an alarm clock, rockets, compass, and some maps. He introduced himself as Captain Paul Boyton, and explained that he was floating down the river from Glendive, Montana to St. Loius, Missouri. He stayed the night at the Fort, and early the next morning White Hawk was among those who watched the adventurer resume his 3500-mile journey down river.

Encouraged by his missionary friend, the Reverend Hall, White Hawk, at fourteen, went to Fort Stevenson to attend the government boarding school. He took the name given him by his father, that of Charles Ward Hoffman, and determined that he would become an educated man. Between the years 1885 and 1890 he attended Santee Normal Training School at Santee, Nebraska. Then he went to Kimball Union Academy at Meridan, New Hampshire, and was graduated from the Academy in 1894.

He accepted a teaching postition at Santee Normal, and while teaching there fell in love with another teacher, a white girl named Carolette Smith. At the end of the school year, he escorted a group of the Fort Berthold students home, and spent his summer at Elbowoods building a comfortable cabin.

On August 1, 1895 he was at Bismarck to meet and marry Miss Smith. By horse and buggy, the newlyweds made the two-day jaunt over the open prairies to their Elbowoods home. For a time, young Hoffman was employed at the Joe Packineau store there.

The next fall, strongly against the advice of friends, Charles and Carolette Hoffman accepted the responsibility of establishing a government day school at Shell Creek village, a community inhabited by the followers of the rebellious Hidatsa chief, Crow-Flies-High.

More than a quarter of a century earlier, this proud and independent chief had led a band of some twenty-five families from the Reservation rather than stay and accept government rations and suffer military indignities they found unbearable. As scouts and hunters in the vicinity of Fort Buford, they managed to make their own living. Finally, however, they were corralled and forced to return to the Reservation; they settled the Shell Creek district.

To Shell Creek Village, Mr. and Mrs. Hoffman came, one week before their school was due to open. Two buildings, each about 24 by 30 feet (and connected by a shed) were in readiness. One building was the schoolhouse; the other the teachers' dwelling.

Shell Creek Day School pupils did not assemble in the schoolroom at the ringing of a school bell. Many young people of school age had married in order to avoid compulsory education. Those who did report without forcible assistance by the Indian policeman, came because a noon meal was to be served regularly by Mrs. Hoffman. For some time, the unschooled patrons of Day School No. 3 considered the food provided by the School the chief benefit of education.

About thirty boys and girls, ranging in age from 6 to 16, attended school that first year (1896-1897). From some of the names entered in the school register for that period can be observed the transition of Indian names to Christian ones:

Bessie, Charles and Cecil Grant: children of Curl Woman and Iron Bull

David Bad Brave: son of Bad Brave

Fanny Daws: Enemy Dog and Cherry Woman

Mary and Rufus Red Feather: Red Feather

Frank and Jessie Birds Bill: Tony Birds Bill

Fannie, Minnie and Ernest Black Hawk: Black Hawk and Mink Woman

Martin and Ralph Levings: Hard Horn

James, Louis and Virginia Drags Wolf: Chief Drags Wolf (son of Crow-Flies-High) and Prairie Dog Woman

Nora and Chester Smith: Long Tail and Beaver Woman

The teachers could not at once begin teaching their charges the Three R's. These children of the open prairies could speak no English, and they must also learn the elementary principles of the white man's civilization before they could be expected to study academic subjects.

The teachers' very first task was to get their pupils adequately clothed. One pupil only, Mark Necklace, came to school in traditional Indian garb — moccasins, beads, long braided hair and buckskin trousers. His father presented him to the schoolmaster, explaining that since this would be his son's last day as an Indian, he wanted him to be attired in his Indian best, for once the boy started to school, he would learn to live and to look like a white man.

Charley Hoffman measured the boys for the clothing to be issued from the Agency headquarters at Elbowoods: shoes, socks, underwear, shirts and trousers. His wife measured the girls, but for shoes and stockings only; the dresses she would teach the little red women to make themselves from gingham provided through the Agency.

His measuring accomplished, Charley went to work on the boys with barber shears and a fine-tooth comb. In her kitchen, Carolette prepared the noon meal. It was carried through the connecting shed and served on the pupils' desks. The Agency, on ration days, doled out such food staples as flour, bacon, salt pork, beans, rice, dried apples, soups, hominy and fresh meat. The food and clothes were transported by wagon from Elbowoods by the Indian policeman, James Hunts Along.

Instruction in the English language eventually got under way. How to sign names, to figure money, and to read and write came in due course.

One of Charley Hoffman's earliest pupils was a deaf boy called "Looking for Something to Eat," and he proved an apt mathematician; he especially delighted in outdoing his fellows in rapid addition contests. A popular school activity was a weekly debate in which the schoolmaster served as judge. Here the boys, with Indian gift for oratory, threshed out many questions. Participants clamored for the privilege of several debates a week.

After preliminary training of six years at the Day School the children were ready for the boarding school at Elbowoods. While most of the parents became quite cooperative in allowing their children to attend the Day School, they set up strenuous objection to their children leaving for a boarding school. It required much coaxing before 90 per cent of the Day School pupils could be recruited for Elbowoods.

Habits the children might readily acquire in the day were difficult to put into practice in homes that were crude log huts with dirt floors and sod roofs, and having as cooking equipment only an old iron kettle, a frying pan, a dripping pan for baking biscuits, and a large spoon and fork.

The boys in short-cropped hair came home to fathers wearing long braids and seeing no value in hair cuts. It seemed to the parents impractical to educate girls who had but one reason for being — to become the squaw of some brave willing to exchange horses for her. Only by very slow degrees did the parents accept the new ways taught to their children by the Hoffmans.

Hoffman himself was of Indian blood, and he could speak the Hidatsa tongue. This gave the Shell Creek people con-

Charles Ward Hoffman,
in 1894

A view of the Shell Creek
Day School, 1926

Thanksgiving Dinner at Shell Creek
Day School, 1929

Indians ready for church, l. to r., Charles Smith, George Parshall, Mark Mato, Four Dance, Conrad Smith, Bear-on-the-Flat, Crows Heart (last of the old-time Mandans)

Photo taken in 1930 shows, from l. to r., Bear-in-the-Water, Honorable James Sinclair, Congressman; Chief Drags Wolf, Pete Shefveland, Ted Sjole.

This snapshot shows a horse painted and ready for a gift presentation at a Fourth of July grass dance, 1930

Jack Lonefight at wheel of early tractor purchased for threshing power by Shell Creek Indians, 1929

Joe Ward's earth lodge — the last such dwelling on the Reservation at Shell Creek Village, 1927

Mr. and Mrs. C. W. Hoffman on their 51st wedding anniversary, August, 1946

Mrs. Hoffman with an old-time friend and co-worker, Dr. Mary McKee, 1940. Dr. McKee died in 1947

fidence in him. And, gradually, as their faith in the native medicine man waned, they reported their ailments to the Hoffmans and were given aid by the Agency physician, Dr. Mary H. McKee. The Hoffmans often assisted with vaccinations.

Reverend C. L. Hall was unable to come to Shell Creek oftener than once a month for preaching services. Hoffman, though he was not ordained, preached regularly at the schoolhouse — using the Hidatsa tongue. And he and Carolette organized a Sunday School.

In the early years, attendance at Sunday preaching services would vary between members of the Wounded Faces clan and members of the Beavers clan. These two factions of the Shell Creek band — one led by Long Bear, the other by Cherries-in-the-Mouth — refused to attend church together. When rumor had it that the Beavers planned to be at the preaching service, the Wounded Faces stayed home — and *vice versa*. With the passing of time, however, these tribal feuds wore thin, and they managed to attend church together.

Among the Day School teachings which the parents found it difficult to accept was medical aid from a white physician. Although faith in the medicine man and their fetishes waned, they still clung to their herb cures. Too, they were reluctant to give up their shrines, their sacred bundles and amulets and their tribal dances. A law restricted these dances to one on the Fourth of July, and a second at Christmas time.

One of the Hidatsa customs which Charley Hoffman, for practical reasons, strongly opposed was the "gift" dance honoring visitors from other tribes.

At one of these Grass Dances, Hidatsa men appeared in traditional finery; some wore deer-tail headdresses and bells, others war bonnets. Each of the painted participants had a song which chronicled his own achievements as warrior or hunter. As he danced and sang, members of his family would bring forth gifts for him to present to the honored guest. Such dances were meant to display the affluence of the host; the gift depended on the resources of the Hidatsa host, and it might be anything from calico to horses.

This custom of putting on a big front frequently would reduce an Hidatsa family to dire need. Logically, Hoffman strove to curb it. The ostentatious giving was a product of the fierce pride in the Hidatsa people, and often they gave lavishly to men of tribes whose resources far surpassed their own.

In 1908, Charley Hoffman was appointed Superintendent of the Fort Berthold Indian Reservation. With the position came the title of "Major." During his period of service, the townsites of Sanish, Van Hook and Parshall, all located in territory originally a part of the Reservation, were surveyed. Major Hoffman did the naming. Van Hook and Parshall honored obscure but trusty mule-skinners who worked with the surveyors. Sanish which nestled in the shadow of Crow-Flies-High Butte, and in time was to be inundated by the waters of the Garrison Dam Reservoir, Hoffman gave a name which, in the Arikara tongue means "Real People."

Hoffman was eminently successful as Superintendent for he had the confidence of the Three Affiliated Tribes. Since he was of Indian background he understood their problems. A man of great moral integrity, of high personal ideals, he had their best interests at heart. Even such uncompliant men as Drags Wolf, Medicine Crow, Makes-the-Dust-Fly, Snarling Wolf and Long Bear esteemed him as a friend and accepted his counsel.

After five years as Superintendent, Hoffman resigned. Then he and Carolette went to Poplar, Montana and taught for a year. They returned to the Shell Creek Day School and his school patrons, those high-spirited followers of Crow-Flies-High bestowed on him their name of veneration: Rising Bear.

After teaching twenty-three years at the Shell Creek Day School and three years at the Independence Day School, Hoffman rounded out his educational work by serving as farm supervisor in the Shell Creek district. Retired in 1933, he had given a total of thirty-seven years to Indian service.

To do him honor, 200 Indians gathered at the Shell Creek

village hall. And the gifts bestowed were not for displaying their own affluance, but to express sincere gratitude to him and his wife for their years of faithful service and friendship. Five Shell Creek Indians — Adlai Stevenson, Four Dance, Roger Brown, Medicine Crow, and Chief Drags Wolf — each stood up to recount the good deeds of their cherished Rising Bear.

The Hoffmans moved to Elmwood Ranch, located seven miles south of Sanish, on the McKenzie County side of the Missouri. Hoffman built a picturesque cabin of cottonwood logs near the home of his son George. There Charley and his wife celebrated their Golden Wedding anniversary.

Carolette died on New Year's Eve, 1950, and Charles Ward Hoffman was left alone in the little cabin situated where the waters of the Big Muddy, impounded by Garrison Dam, rise to flood the fertile benchlands and the valley that Hoffman roamed and loved for so long.

But wherever the gentle and cultured Rising Bear may abide, he will carry with him the memory of fifty years of happy companionship with his beloved Carolette, of teaching together many years in a little North Dakota schoolhouse.

The name of Charles Ward Hoffman will long outlive him. Red men and white will long honor the memory of one whose humble labors made ready the way for those who follow after.

24 "Long-Haired" Morgan

ONE of the most unusual individuals ever to reside in what is now Mercer County was "Long-Haired" Morgan Spencer.

His cabin on Spring Creek was built of logs and rocks and sod. Within the crude structure was a trap-door opening into a 300-foot tunnel that led to a clump of bushes on the bank of the creek. None of his neighbors was ever able to learn why Long-Haired Morgan dug this tunnel.

Well-educated and accustomed to the refinements of civilization, Spencer chose the life of a trapper. He wore his black hair in a flowing mane, and always carried a bowie-knife. He spent so much of his time throwing this knife that he developed an amazing marksmanship.

In 1885 he established a postoffice named Morganville, on the old Bismarck-Fort Stevenson stage route and was himself the postmaster. A few years later, he disappeared.

Then suddenly in the early 90s, he reappeared in North Dakota. He was with a traveling show, and Mercer county neighbors now paid admission to see Long-Haired Morgan throw his bowie knife.

His appearance was something to behold. He wore a much-fringed buckskin coat, high-topped gleaming black boots, and a bright red bandana to bind the flowing black mane.

Long-Haired Morgan's act called for a partner. Against the planked wall in the show booth there stood an attractive woman, her arms extended horizontally. She was, indeed, the performer's new wife.

Morgan would step back eight paces from the planked wall. From a table, he selected one of the eighteen bowie knives lying there. With dramatically accurate aim he hurled the long-bladed weapon into the wall — barely missing the woman's body. Again and again this was done until eighteen bowie knives roughly outlined the body of his wife. Then Long-Haired Morgan turned ceremoniously about and bowed to the awed spectators.

The show moved on, and on. But finally word drifted back to Mercer County that on a certain day one of the eighteen knives failed of its aim — and ended the life of Long-Haired Morgan's trusting partner.

25 *The Undiscovered Poet of the West*

ONE day at Maxbass, end of the newly constructed railway spur, a man climbed aboard the train with a suitcase in one hand and a garden hoe in the other. While the chill wind blew outside, he settled himself comfortably in a coach seat, placing the worn hoe close beside him.

Passengers eyed the new arrival wonderingly. One, unable to contain his curiosity, leaned into the aisle and questioned, "What, Sir, may I ask, are you doing with a hoe at this time of the year?"

The man with the hoe smiled indulgently. "Well, Sir," he replied, "I'm going down to Minot, and since politics are warming up down there, I may find it necessary to do a little weeding." A moment later he added confidentially, "Also, I intend to have my hoe silver-plated — I am very fond of it."

The facetious answer was characteristic of the man, James J. Somers. Originally a Minneapolis grocer, he settled on a claim near Maxbass at the turn of the century. Lacking equipment for more extensive tilling, he did his farming with a hoe.

James J. Somers, the "Undiscovered Poet of the West"

Photo by courtesy of Minot State Teachers College

Mark "Lazarus" Hansen

North Dakota Historical Society photo

The lonely bachelor oftentimes expressed his heart longings in rhyme — lyrics which the neighbors appreciated. He was hospitable and his prairie home was the scene of many an old-time party. Eventually, there was a bride to share his life with the hoe.

When he had proved up his homestead, Jim Somers took his wife and his hoe and went back to Minneapolis to live. There, in 1913, he published a collection of his prairie verses, entitling it *Jim's Western Gems by the Undiscovered Poet of the West.*

Representative of his prairie "poetry" was "Along the Minot Trail":

I am one of the pioneers
Of North Dakota state.
At Hill's request I came out west
In search of real estate.
I filed along the Cut Bank Creek,
Just forty miles from rail,
And I started farming with a hoe,
Along the Minot Trail.

There wasn't any Westhope then;
We had no hopes at all;
It was a long time after
That I heard about Mohall.
We had to go to Bottineau
Or Minot for our mail,
Until we started Renville
Along the Minot trail.

Sometimes we'd stop at Christopher's,
More times at Half-Breed Lake;
Sometimes they'd have no room for us
At the place we tried to make.
We'd drive on to some other shack,
Through rain, through snow, or hail;
I have had the blues from wading sloughs
Along the Minot trail.

And when we'd reach our old sod shacks,
With none to greet us there,
A meal of bacon and dough-jacks
We quickly would prepare.
We'd think about our old sweethearts,
And hoped we would not fail
To win a wife to share our life
Along the Minot trail.

The only fuel we knew about
Was prairie hay and straw.
From November until April,
We never had a thaw.
I often thought I'd rather be
In some good warm jail
While twisting hay both night and day
Along the Minot trail.

And when the snow would disappear,
The gophers would begin —
They'd eat up everything we sowed,
And then we'd sow again.
If I could scheme some new device
To kill the Flicker-Tail,
I might stand a show with my old hoe
Along the Minot trail.

The flying ants were another pest
That would drive a man back East;
They'd light on you by millions,
And upon you they would feast.
Your clothes would not protect you —
Right through them they would sail.
They would sting and chew you black and blue
Along the Minot trail.

But we've railroads now on every side,
And rumors of some more;
And people, hunting after land,
Are coming by the score.
And when I go to Minot now,
I go around by rail;
But I don't forget the friends I met
Along the Minot trail.

26 "Lazarus" Hanson

DURING the summer of 1931, newspapers over North Dakota reported the death of Mark L. Hanson, a transient typesetter who had worked on most of the newspapers in the state. The report had come from Idaho that Hanson had been struck by a speeding automobile.

Many editors, remembering the honesty and the kindness of the man, wrote tear-jerking obituaries. A few featured the fact that he had set type for some of James W. Foley's first poems published in the Bismarck *Tribune*.

But when spring returned to North Dakota in 1932, Mark L. Hanson also returned, and in the flesh.

On learning that he had been reported as dead and buried, the genial "Lazarus" (as he was dubbed), exulted in his resurrected life and began the hobby of collecting his own obituaries.

He rambled over North Dakota and portions of nearby states, working a month on this newspaper, a short time on that, visiting another briefly — and managing always to obtain clippings of his own death. When, in 1941, death really came, his collection of Mark Hanson obituaries totaled nearly 200.

27 "Wrong Side Up"

*H*ALF a mile east of New Salem, beside the highway, is the "Wrong Side Up" monument. And in the town, in an old house with a porch extending over the sidewalk, lives 90-year-old "Wrong Side Up" Christiansen whose portrait hangs in the gallery of the North Dakota Agricultural College Hall of Fame.

Back of these related facts there lies a tale.

In 1881 when John Christiansen was 19, he came to America. As he worked as a farm laborer in Wisconsin, he dreamed of owning a farm, but he feared he could never save enough for one from his earnings. So when he heard that the German Evangelical Church in Chicago was organizing a company of German immigrants to start a colony in western Dakota Territory, he managed the required membership fee of $20 and joined.

The colonists and their families, with all their personal belongings, were crowded into a half dozen immigrant cars. There were no Pullman luxuries for these early settlers — they slept on double bunks made of rough planks.

John's passage was on a freight train, in a car with his team of horses, a supply of hay and oats, his knocked-down wagon, and property belonging to three of his friends. At Jamestown, during a train stop, he got off and bought a breaking plow from a farmer, and that he tied to the top of his freight car.

He arrived at Mandan, April 4, 1883, and continued on ahead of the immigrant train scheduled to come a day later. John's train came to a stop at "New Salem" — at that time a platted town that existed only in the dreams and hopes of men, a town of prairie grass greening and pasque flowers lifting lavender cups to the spring sun. And there John's horses were taken from the car, led over planks laid across to a cutbank. Then the train crew dumped the other contents of his car in haphazard fashion on both sides of the tracks. This done, the men climbed back into the caboose, the locomotive wheezed off toward the setting sun, and John Christiansen stood there alone on the open prairie.

It was cold. Snow still lay in great drifts in the coulees. Dark clouds came "over the hill where the schoolhouse now stands."

John tethered his horses to wagon wheels. Darkness shrouded him while he searched vainly for his tent. Coyotes on nearby hills pointed noses to the threatening sky and howled. Remembering the ferocious wolves of European forests, John sat there stiff from cold and fear through the long night.

At dawn, the immigrant train arrived with the other citizens of New Salem. But it stopped only long enough for John's three friends to get off, then steamed ahead several miles to the nearest siding. Here the immigrants were left until crew men could construct a siding for their cars at New Salem.

After one day, this New Salem siding was ready, and all the colonists returned. The immigrant cars served them as living quarters until they had built the "Immigrant House," a structure 30 by 40 feet. Into this three-room dwelling piled entire families. Shortly, stowaway immigrants crawled out from the walls of the Immigrant House — bedbugs from Minnesota camps secreted on the pine boards and timbers. The New Salem colonists were dismayed.

Together the colonists built a barn for their pastor, the Reverend Henry Gyr — the barn's hayloft to serve as the clergyman's personal quarters, the space below to quarter his cow and five horses. That same year, they built also the first New Salem church. When it was completed, the colonists were not only dismayed but chagrined as well, for

John Christiansen

Elizabeth Preston Anderson

Mrs. C. E. Webster when she was North Dakota's first telephone operator

the lumber used came from the same Minnesota camp which had supplied material for the Immigrant House. Christiansen recalls that the vermin were no heathen tribe, but faithful in attending services. "We could see them crawling across the ceiling — coming down the walls."

During the first summer, the colonists scattered about on homesteads where they built small frame shanties. And John, with the only breaking plow in the territory, kept busy turning sod — an acre of land on each homestead.

While he was one day engaged with turning up sod on his own homestead, he caught sight of a strange caravan coming down the old Keogh Trail. When he reached the end of his furrow, he could see that the travelers were two Indian families, transporting their belongings by travois.

John was excited for he had never seen Indians before. The two Indian fathers, followed by a youth of fifteen, approached him. And he could hardly believe his own ears when one of the fathers greeted him with "How, John."

He did not yet know that Indians of that day addressed any and all white men as "John." He was so flustered that the only reply he could think to make was, "How, John!"

With great solemnity this Indian stopped and began to turn slabs of sod back into the furrow, carefully patting each one into place again, and repeating as he did so, something in his own tongue. The Indian youth turned to John Christiansen and said in English, "He say 'Wrong side up'."

The New Salem colonists planted grain upon the acres of sod turned wrong side up, but seven lean years of crop failure followed. Many settlers left in discouragement. Several winters, John went to northern Minnesota lumber camps to earn money so that he could buy horses, to help make reality his stubborn dream of a farm home of his own.

Often through those early years of drouth, John pondered the words of the Indian . . . Perhaps he was wise, after all, this Indian who supposedly knew nothing about farming. Surely he who had roamed this prarie land always, knew it better than did immigrant settlers.

Why not raise dairy cows on the prairie hills where the sod still lay right side up? John began with a common red cow, later obtained a pure-bred Holstein. His Holstein herd grew, and John prospered. He became the first farmer in North Dakota to keep an official dairy record. His accomplishments as a dairyman became known over the state, and he was elected to the North Dakota Hall of Fame. Farmers and dairymen drove hundreds of miles to inspect John Christiansen's dairy farm, and over and over, he told them the story of "Wrong Side Up."

When drouth years had continued, John's neighbors also considered the words of the Indian, and brought cattle to graze upon the grassy hills instead of turning more sod wrong side up. Prosperity followed as New Salem became one of the leading dairy centers in the state. And in gratitude to that Indian's counsel, the "Wrong Side Up" monument was erected on the spot where John that day was breaking sod.

28 *Crusading Lady*

FROM her hotel window, Elizabeth Preston looked out and saw upon the ground below the inert figure of a young man. The morning sun beat down upon him; flies crawled over his face.

Just beyond him was the back door of the town saloon. Several times since coming to Page to teach, Elizabeth had seen that back door swung open and a drunken man tossed out — to lie on the ground, like this young fellow, until consciousness returned.

An hour later, Elizabeth stood before the bright, eager-faced children in her classroom, and wondered which of her boys might grow up to have their lives shackled by liquor. Suddenly she knew her call to service — a call that was to make her one of the most remembered women in North Dakota. In time, newspapers throughout the state would refer to her simply as "Elizabeth" and readers would need no further identification.

When a group of women met at the Page schoolhouse to form a sewing society, Elizabeth Preston persuaded them to organize a Woman's Christian Temperance Union instead. She was elected president of the group. Public meetings were held on the first Sunday of each month and they proved popular gatherings for the townspeople. Among those who sang in the WCTU choir was young L. B. Hanna who later became governor of North Dakota.

Elizabeth led her group in a total abstinence pledge-signing campaign, organized an anti-saloon crusade, and soon had the satisfaction of seeing the Page saloon closed.

That was the beginning of a career which was to see Elizabeth serving 40 years as president of the North Dakota WCTU, 20 years as national WCTU recording secretary, and a level-headed leader in the woman suffrage movement in the state.

When the North Dakota WCTU was organized at Yankton, South Dakota in 1889, Elizabeth was elected as assistant organizer and evangelistic superintendent of the new organization. A woman of energy and of unstinting devotion to her cause, her work evoked such approval and respect that she was elected state president in 1893 and served continuously in that office until she retired in 1933.

The prohibition clause of the state constitution had passed by a small majority of 1159 votes. Elizabeth, therefore, was convinced that her organization must guard vigilantly the law and its enforcement. She believed the most effective agency for this purpose was a live local WCTU group in every town where it was possible to organize one.

And so, during those pioneer years, she traveled almost constantly over the state, organizing and encouraging the local Unions. Oxen, mule team, bronco, Indian pony, bicycle, hand-car, caboose and day coach served her as means of transportation. Her Blickensderfer typewriter traveled with her much of the time to help in keeping up with official correspondence.

One particular trip she has never been able to forget. She had hired a livery team and driver to take her to her next appointment. Her foes, with malice aforethought, treated this driver generously to whiskey, bundled him in a big fur coat and had him in the front seat of the sleigh when the WCTU leader was ready to leave. A short way out of town, Elizabeth realized the man's inebriate condition. Fortunately, the weather was of sobering below zero temperature, and the man kept a sufficiently tight rein on the spirited horses that Bottineau was reached safely and in good time.

A temperance crusader's path, Elizabeth early discovered, was not strewn with prairie roses. At Forman, in 1891, a minister allowed Elizabeth and her WCTU colleagues to meet in his church on week days, only after the women of the congregation threatened him with reprisal. Next Sunday he preached pointedly from the text: "Let the women keep silence in the churches" and on the Sunday after that: "It is a shame for a woman to speak in church."

However, there was a young Forman minister, James Anderson, who not only attended the WCTU meetings but openly encouraged the women in their endeavors. He had persuasions other than those on temperance, too, for some years later, in a "White Ribbon" wedding, he and Elizabeth Preston were made man and wife.

At one North Dakota church, a stocky red-faced Scotchman stamped indignantly out of the church when he beheld Elizabeth — a woman! — mount the pulpit. In another church, an emissary from the "wets" staggered up the long center aisle to the front pew, and began to heckle the state WCTU president as she spoke. Elizabeth addressed him quietly, explaining that she had something to say and that he could have the floor after she had concluded. That would be fair, would it not? He nodded his head and fell silent. He had drowsed into near sleep when an officer arrived and ushered him from the meeting.

As she traveled over North Dakota in those pre-hotel-inspection days, Elizabeth spent many sleepless nights in hotel rooms infested with vermin. Most of the time she was tendered the hospitality of private homes. One of the most memorable occasions was in a meticulously clean but most sparsely furnished home. The one rug in the house was brought and placed before Elizabeth's bed. At the little rural church where the WCTU meetings were held, her hostess, dressed in calico, read a scholarly paper. The afternoon meeting concluded, this woman drove home in her wagon to see to the needs of her own — and her hospitalized sister's — children, milked seven cows, then returned to the church to help serve supper there.

Elizabeth made her first visit to the state legislative halls in 1893. Bismarck was then a straggling western town, its main street facing the Northern Pacific tracks. Liquor was easy to obtain in the capital city. In the legislature, a battle royal waged over the resubmission of the prohibition amendment. And liquor interests, Elizabeth found, bribed any legislator who could be bribed. A personal friend of hers found in his desk one morning a roll of bills covering the exact amount of a heavy mortgage on his land.

One year when the vote for resubmission was expected to be very close, a certain Senator, a Prohibitionist politically, but a man given to drink, became intoxicated. Elizabeth sent a page for him. When the Senator arrived, he greeted her with, "Mish Preshton, I'm all right! You'll shee I'm all right when we vote on reshubmission!" And he cast his vote for prohibition.

In 1895, resubmission was defeated by only one vote. Greatly alarmed, Elizabeth enlisted the aid of all the prominent citizens who espoused prohibition, and the North Dakota Enforcement League was thus formed. R. B. Griffith, Grand Forks merchant, served as its president. From 1911 to 1925, when the Reverend F. L. "Shoot to Kill" Watkins was enforcement superintendent, bootleggers found North Dakota a hazardous place in which to operate.

Watkins often disguised himself with a mustache, or dressed like a tramp in order to track down whiskey runners. It never became necessary for him to kill a man, but bootleggers knew he was a crack shot with his Winchester rifle. A gang of Minneapolis rum runners accordingly offered $15,000 as reward to anyone who would liquidate the fearless minister. On August 30, 1921, a man by the name of Barney Bussen was shot and wounded when he was mistaken for Watkins. Nobody ever "got" the Reverend Watkins; he died at Mandan July 8, 1940 at the age of seventy-one.

When, in the early part of the century, the North Dakota WCTU was at the height of its power, it secured passage of laws which provided for physical education and an annual temperance day in the public schools, and penalty for Sabbath breaking; laws which prohibited impure literature, Sunday baseball, Sunday theater, gambling, the public drinking cup, cigarette smoking in public dining halls, and the sale of Copenhagen snuff and cigarettes and cigarette papers. After World War I, several of these laws were repealed. And during the Franklin Delano Roosevelt administration came the repeal of national prohibition.

On having someone remark, "It's too bad that you should see the results of your life work swept away," Mrs. Anderson has replied: "It was well worth all the effort, to have the privilege of bringing up our own family in a prohibition state and to see the effect of a saloonless environment on a whole generation of young people." She has, too, the satisfaction of knowing that North Dakota did not vote for the repeal of the 18th Amendment, and that for 47 years the prairie state was dry.

Around a public figure as indomitable as Elizabeth Preston Anderson, many myths arose. One of the most widely-circulated stories was the Dan Sullivan legend, following a resubmission fight in the early 90s. Dan Sullivan was an East Grand Forks, Minnesota saloonkeeper who enjoyed a bonus trade slaking the thirst of customers from the other side of the Red River; he was presumably interested in keeping North

Dakota prohibition on the statute books. A minister astonished Mrs. Anderson by asking her if it was true that one year when resubmision had again been defeated, she had embraced Dan Sullivan and presented him with a beautiful bouquet in appreciation of his help in keeping North Dakota dry.

The WCTU crusader was awake to other needed reforms in her state. For a quarter of a century she worked vigorously for the interests of woman suffrage, without attaining the goal. Then in 1917 she secured a copy of the Illinois municipal and presidential suffrage law and had Robert M. Pollock, a Fargo attorney, examine it. A bill for substantially the same law was introduced in the North Dakota senate and within ten days had passed both the houses and was signed by Governor Lynn J. Frazier. North Dakota, thereby, was one of the states that already had municipal and presidential suffrage when the 19th Amendment of the Federal Constitution was adopted.

In her memoirs, Mrs. Anderson has recorded a surprising revelation concerning a near-victory for woman suffrage:

> *In 1893, Senator Stevens of Dickey County introduced a suffrage bill in the North Dakota Senate. It was at this time that I made my first visit to the State Capitol, to work for this measure, and against resubmission. The bill passed the Senate and came up in the House for final action on the last day of the session. I was invited to speak on the measure; the roll call which followed, showed that it had passed by constitutional majority. Then came a most spectacular fight. The Speaker of the House refused to sign the bill. Governor Shortridge let it be known that if the bill came to him, he would sign it, and that he believed that as it had passed both the Senate and the House, it would go into effect without the signature of the Speaker of the House.*
>
> *Men were placed in the halls and outside the doors of the Governor's office to prevent the bill*

reaching him. For several hours the bill was "lost."

The Senate, which had got possession of the bill, voted down several requests that they return it to the House; Senator LaMoure moved, and it was carried, that the president of the Senate be instructed to sign no more House bills until the Speaker of the House had signed the Senate bill. Legislation was thus blocked, and for a time pandemonium reigned. Many important measures were pending, and as the hour of final adjournment drew near, in order to save them, the Senate voted to return the bill to the House. The House voted to expunge the records, so there is nothing in the Journal of the House to show that woman suffrage passed both houses in 1893.

When Elizabeth Preston Anderson retired as state WCTU president the Fargo *Forum* editorialized:

All in all, while the cause of prohibition by mandate of law is at a low ebb today, Mrs. Anderson has made a notable contribution to the life of North Dakota, for who will gainsay the fact that she has added something material to the moral fabric of North Dakota. Those who have opposed her will be the first to acknowledge the fact that she has been a great fighter for the cause she embraced — a cause to which no day has passed in all the forty years of her presidency of the WCTU except that some part of it was dedicated to its ahcievement.

When her pastor husband also retired, there followed for the two of them "six, almost incredibly happy, restful years" in which they divided their time between the Memorial Home Community at Penney Farms, Florida, and their summer home, Oak Lodge, near Detroit Lakes, Minnesota.

With advancing years, Mrs. Anderson's eyesight began to fail, and her husband became "eyes" for her until his death in 1941. Now ninety-three, this veteran crusader lives with a stepson, Dr. Howard Anderson, at Miles City, Montana

— and his wife Margaret now serves as eyes and ears to the intrepid lady who lives in a "house of clay growing dark and silent." She has learned to read by Braille, types letters to an "inner circle of friends grown much smaller . . . but the great cloud of witnesses over there has grown larger." Her joyful spirit is epitomized in a verse of poetry she often repeats to herself:

> When thou, clay cottage, fallest, I'll immerse
> My long-cramped spirit in the universe.
> Through uncomputed silences of space
> I shall yearn upwards toward the leaning Face.
> The Heavens shall roll back for me,
> As Moses monarched the dividing sea.
> This body is my house; it is not I.
> Triumphant in this faith I live and die.
> —FREDERICK LAWRENCE KNOWLES

29 North Dakota's First Hello Girl

ON a Sunday early in 1881, young Bella Thomson left the First Baptist Church of Fargo and started homeward to "Quality Flats." Mr. John B. Inman joined her and directly began telling her about his telephone exchange, then Fargo's newest enterprise. He asked her, "Bella, would you be interested in working for me as telephone operator?"

The girl was surprised. In those days, few young ladies took jobs down town, so she replied, "Well, I'll have to ask Mother and see what she says."

Mrs. Thomson consented, so in March of that year, 16-year-old Bella began work at the first telephone switchboard in North Dakota — in an attic room of the old Headquarters Hotel.

From the one small round window of that room, Bella looked down on the wooden sidewalks along the muddy, or dusty, thoroughfare of Broadway. Toward Moorhead lay the single track of the Northern Pacific.

Bella had no headphone to use. The mouthpiece was stationary, and in order to answer a call she had to take the ear phone off a hook. About fifty Fargo business firms and residences were connected to this pioneer switchboard by means of iron fence wire strung over the tops of buildings. The first farm residence to install a telephone connected to the Fargo switchboard was that of Mr. James Holes. This residence still stands at 1233 Broadway.

After a year and a half of work at the switchboard, Bella went back to high school. While she was at school, the telephone center was moved from the Hotel to the second floor of the Fire Hall on NP Avenue. Here, in the makeshift quarters, Bella returned to work; the telephone business was growing — so now she had two assistants, Cora Cooper and Margaret Wallace. The room was large and drafty, and though the pot-bellied stove in its center roared and reddened, the switchboard girls were often chilled. More comfortable quarters were obtained a year later in the new Hageman Block.

One day, with her older sister Mary, Bella went to the old red, white and blue Continental Hotel where Mary was to help organize the "Toxopholite Society," an archery club. Of more lasting interest to Bella was a young man, Charles E. Webster, she met there that day. The two were married in 1885.

Now 89 years of age, Mrs. Webster continues to live in Fargo. Besides being the state's first "Hello Girl," she also has the distinction of being a charter member of the first Federated Women's club organized in North Dakota.

The Fargo switchboard was the first one in the state, but the first telephone installed in North Dakota was one which connected two Grandin Farms in Traill County. Mr. J. L. Grandin, one of the owners of these bonanza farms, had seen

Alexander Graham Bell demonstrate his telephone invention at the Philadelphia Exposition in 1876, and immediately purchased two instruments. These were installed on the farms, and were in use the following year.

30 "Tree-Tops" Klingensmith

FLORENCE was nine years old when she first saw an airplane. "Some day," she pledged herself, "I'll get in an airplane, and I'll go up above the tree tops where the birds are!"

In 1919, when she had reached thirteen, she learned to drive an automobile — and developed an insatiable desire to pull down on the gas lever. Within a few years she and her brother George built themselves a racer, from a second-hand car; horses shied to the roadside when those two Gundersons zoomed over rural Moorhead and Fargo roads.

But Florence and George wanted something that would give greater speed than a home-made roadster, and so managed to buy a motorcycle. They were making 70 miles an hour on it one day when the front tire blew out, sending Florence sailing through the air. She retrieved herself in one bruised piece, but decided that her next flight would not be by way of a motorcycle.

A fair that came to Fargo had along a commercial airplane and Florence lost no time in distributing enough posters to earn herself a free ride in the flying-machine. But this first ride failed to do all for her that she had so long anticipated, and her interest in flying went into brief eclipse.

When she was a Junior in the Moorhead high school, her parents went to live on a farm in northern Minnesota and Florence quit school to share in the new life. But life on the

Photo by courtesy of Mrs. W. D. Hartman, Fargo

Florence "Tree Tops" Klingensmith

farm was not for Florence, so she went to Fargo where she clerked in a store for a time. Next she tried a nurse-girl job and soon quit that for something she really enjoyed — driving a truck for a dry-cleaning establishment.

Then Charles Lindbergh made his memorable non-stop flight across the Atlantic, and Florence — Mrs. Klingensmith now — was infected by the flying virus. And after the early North Dakota flier, Mr. E. M. Canfield, took her for a ride high above the tree tops, she knew of a surety that to fly was her life's mission.

She took a ground course at Hanson Aviation School in Fargo. Canfield gave her some training and, on June 22, 1928, let her go, solo, in his plane. From then on Florence Klingensmith's life was inseparable from flying.

Her excitement over having tried her own wings was such that her flying friends started calling her "Tree-Tops" and the name stuck. And now, she wanted to know what it would be like to make a parachute jump.

She bought a parachute and Canfield took her up over Hector airport, outside of Fargo. She made her first jump from an altitude of 1700 feet. As she descended, she pendulumed considerably and was knocked unconscious when she hit the ground.

But only two weeks later, Tree-Tops was at Brainerd, Minnesota to make her second jump. This time she escaped accident. On the following Fourth of July she jumped twice at Bismarck.

She went for a month's course in aviation to Moline, Illinois. There she met several top fliers, among them the noted aviatrix, Mrs. Phoebe Omlie.

Returned to Fargo, Tree-Tops set about getting a Monocoupe, such as the one Mrs. Omlie flew. She canvassed Fargo business men, telling them how she would advertise Fargo with an airplane — if they would provide her with one. "I'll risk my neck," she would say, "if you'll risk your money."

Six men financed the purchase of the plane "Miss Fargo"; and on April 19, 1929, Tree-Tops settled the new monoplane on the Hector flying field.

She was North Dakota's first licensed woman flier, and was only 23 years old when she performed the first flying stunt that brought her national attention.

By eight o'clock on that morning of April 19, 1930, cars lined the road near Hector airport for almost two miles. The show Tree-Tops had promised was an exhibition of looping-the-loop.

At 9:06 a.m. the "Miss Fargo" took off. At 9:18 Tree-Tops went into the first of the 143 loops she was to accomplish. One hour and 13 minutes later she settled the small plane upon the ground, and a crowd of spectators surged across the field to cheer the daring young aviatrix.

Tree-Tops had set an unofficial world's record for women by besting — by almost a hundred — the 46 loops made by Mildred Kauffman of St. Louis, Missouri. Only a few months later, however, Miss Laura Ingalls of New York became the champion when she turned her plane over 980 consecutive times.

Tree-Tops could not let that record go unchallenged. At Minneapolis, on June 21, 1931, before a throng of 25,000 spectators, she looped her plane until she reached a total of 1,078 times. During the 4½ hours of flight she had made four loops a minute — and had come within 355 loops of the world's record set for men by Charles "Speed" Holman.

After this she did exihibition flying in air shows over the nation. Many thousands thrilled to her daring and her surpassing skill in handling an airplane.

She competed in the international air races at Chicago, and, on Sunday, September 4, 1933, placed second in the women's 30-mile race. The following day she was the only woman to enter the $10,000 Phillips competition.

For this race she was to use a plane owned by a Jackson, Michigan man, a lightweight plane whose original motor had been replaced by one of double horsepower.

Tree-Tops was 60 miles on her way in the 100-mile race, and swinging closer to the pylons than any of her competitors risked doing, when the fabric ripped from a wing of her plane.

The grandstand's thousands of eyes now followed only one plane. They could see that Tree-Tops sought frantically for a place to land without endangering the crowds below her. She made her way, at an altitude of about 300 feet, to a vacant nursery field, where the plane suddenly nose-dived as though its pilot had fainted and fallen against the stick.

It was instant death for Florence Klingensmith. Her body was brought to Fargo where many fellow fliers and hundreds of townsfolks paid her final tribute. She was buried at Oak Mound Cemetery, near Moorhead.

31 "Dinna Forget Your Peat!"

*E*ARLY that summer of 1943, Dr. James Grassick had Christmas in his heart, and busied himself writing the little Christmas booklet sent to greet an ever-expanding list of friends.

The many packets of books were ready for mailing when the 93-year-old physician was taken to a Grand Forks hospital where on December 19 he breathed his last. Contained in the final paragraph of that final Christmas message from James Grassick, was a sentence which summed up the spirit of the man's life: "Enough, if we are permitted to peer through the mist, catch a glimpse of the stars beyond and point the upward way."

A small boy in new kilt of homespun and knitted tam stood ready for his first day of school.

"Dinna forget your peat!" reminded his mother.

In that Aberdeenshire, Scotland glen where the Grassicks lived, it was the custom for every pupil to carry with him each morning a chunk of peat for the school fire. "And thus it was

Dr. James Grassick

Captain Edward E. Heerman

North Dakota Historical Society photo

that I began my education by doing my bit for the common weal," Dr. Grassick wrote in one of his Christmas books. "As I entered school and deposited my peat at the door, I got a feeling of pride that has never quite left me."

After graduation — in 1885 — from the medical school of the University of Michigan, the young physician secured work as a deckhand on a lake freighter to earn passage to Duluth. The Red River Valley was the *Eldorado* beckoning him west. Arrived at Duluth, he set out — carpetbag in hand — for Fargo, Dakota Territory, and walked the entire distance. From that point he began search for a settlement that he felt would be the place to hang out his doctor's shingle.

Abroad on the prairie, famished and tired, he made his way to a threshing rig with cookcar nearby. But when he politely asked the cook for something to eat, that burly fellow brandished a skillet at him and shouted, "We don't feed tramps here."

So James Grassick, M. D., tightened his belt and walked on. By mid-afternoon as he approached a settler's cabin, he met a young woman and her toddling child. He observed a cow picketed near the cabin.

He asked for a drink of milk, but the woman did not understand his request until he pointed to the cow, then went through the motions of drinking. Then the Norwegian woman's face lit with comprehension. "*Kom ind!*" she invited, and opened the door of her house. With hospitable haste she set before him bread and butter and a pitcher of milk and bade him, "*Vaer saa god!*"

Thus was Dr. James Grassick welcomed to the community of Buxton where he was to practice medicine for the next twenty years.

As his special "bit for the common weal," he early started to battle the scourge of tuberculosis. When the North Dakota Tuberculosis Association was organized in 1909, he was elected its president. He headed the group continuously until 1928 when he forswore the honor, and became president *emeritus*. That same year, a fresh-air and nutrition camp for children was established on Lake Isabel near Dawson, and it was named in his honor. For many years, he edited the official publication, *The Pennant,* and brought its circulation up to four thousand copies.

Dr. Grassick served three terms as State Superintendent of Public Health, and at one time was state president of the North Dakota Medical Association. In 1905, he moved to Grand Forks where he was to practice until the time of his retirement.

At Christmas his affectionate heart always wanted to give something special to his friends, something that would help each of them to "catch a glimpse of the stars beyond and point the upward way." It was this desire that prompted him to send out each year for nearly half a century the little Christmas books that gave so much delight.

Occasionally, these little books would narrate experiences that had befallen the Doctor. One such incident was the time his sleigh stuck in a snow-clogged coulee. He loosened his horses to take care of themselves. Then he set out in the blizzard's snow-filled darkness to seek shelter. He stumbled upon the railway track, then struggled down its course against the storm, and found he must struggle too against a mounting desire to lie down and sleep. He was at the point of exhaustion when he caught a solitary sound — the braying of a mule. Desperately, he struggled in the direction of that sound. A few rods only, and he fell against a cabin wall. Locating the door, he pounded upon it with his last strength.

The man known as "One-Hundred-and-One" — because of a fondness for the card game of that name — helped him into the warm cabin. Grassick reeled to the floor. When he revived, he found One-Hundred-and-One rubbing his hands, the wife Sigrid ready with hot coffee.

Ole, the mule, did not go unrewarded for that life-saving bray; the Doctor later presented him with a generous sack of corn.

His first year at Buxton, the Doctor joined other bachelors in the community in making a unique presentation at the first

Sunday School observance of Children's Day. His record of the incident describes the gift and giving of:

> *A beer keg, covered with calico having bright conventional figures, giving it the appearance at a distance of a rare antique that might have graced the palace of an oriental prince. It made a substantial vase. In this the wild flowers, ferns and grasses of the prairie were arranged, as artfully as the complex ideas of their gatherers would permit. When completed this unique thing was gorgeous in color, rich in fragrance and imposing in size. Forming a procession the self-appointed delegation marched to the schoolhouse and without announcing their arrival, entered, carried their offering up the aisle and placed it on the stand that served as desk, pulpit and altar. Underneath it they placed a placard with the legend: "A tribute from the bachelors to the children."*

In his booklet entitled *The Paisley Shawl*, Dr. Grassick tells of returning to his native glen in Scotland and visiting in a "wee hoose amang the heather" with one of the dearest of his childhood friends. This aged master weaver, at Grassick's request, tells about a Paisley shawl he had woven in his youth. And in the telling, the prairie physician hears again his cherished old friend's philosophy of life — a philosophy Grassick had adopted for his own.

> *"It is three score years and mair sin' it came frae the loom, and though I say it mysel', it was a fine ane. Ae day I was in the shop workin' awa to feenish a job I had in the loom when wha should come in but my maister wi' a fine ledy by his side. I saw by her looks she was mair than ordinar', sai I stoppit the shuttle and doffed my bonnet.*
>
> *"She came ower by me an' inspeckit my wark an' then said to my maister, 'I'll take this one,' pointing towards my loom. It made my heart thump to hear it. But when she came by me and handed me twa half*

crowns I was near beside mysel'. That nicht, it was in everybody's mou' that the Queen had been buyin' shawls to gae to her gentry friends, an' maybe I wasna' a proud man to ken that ane o' mine had been selected! Weel, I was courtin' my Meg then — an' it came into my head to mak' her a shawl like the ane I made for the Ledy, an' that's it, and there isna' the mara o't outside o' Balmoral! Noo dinna ye think I ken somethin' o' the makin' o't?"

The old man reached over and with his outstretched wizened fingers took hold of a corner of the shawl, held it up to the light, trembling but smiling, as he said:

"Aye, there's wark for ye! There's care intilt, an' skill intilt, an' heart intilt, an' luve intilt — an' that's what counts the maist."

After saying this he stood up seemingly more erect than usual. His eyes glistened and his lips were compressed. In spirit he was again in his prime and felt the surge of honest work coursing through his veins. Raising a hand and pointing to the product of his labors of long ago he said:

"Look at it. There isna' a wrang thread in it. When a man puts the best that is in him into his day's work and is honest wi' himself, he can look the warl' in the e'e an' no flinch, an' when he has finished his stint an' is restin' in the gloamin', an' the shadows are creepin' on, he needna' fear, for it is written, 'The laborer is worthy o' his hire.' Aye, there's a bonnie promise an' I'm takin the Maister at His word. Hire? I wonder — but no, it will be a' I deserve an' mair."

32 Captain of the Minnie-H

TODAY grass-grown marshes stretch for miles where, in 1882, Captain Edward E. Heerman beheld Devil's Lake, that body of water described by Pat Donan as "a majestic inland sea, christened in honor of the patron saint of American politicians."

As Heerman stood there by the lake, new hope surged through him. For years he had piloted steamers on the Mississippi and Chippewa rivers, and he had been a builder of river boats. River freighting was profitable in the years when settlers flooded the great western wilderness, but now, with railways spanning the plains, the era of profitable river navigation was coming to an abrupt end.

Heerman was confident that, here on the placid prairie-land lake, he could establish a thriving boat busines. The great irregular body of water then reached more than thirty miles in length, was a third of that distance at its widest point. The region was settling rapidly, towns were springing up. The ambitious village of Wamduska on nearby Stump Lake already boasted a 70-room hotel. Homesteaders had found Devil's Lake to be a fisherman's paradise — they harpooned fish with pitchforks and hauled their catch away by wagonloads. A boat on the lake could be of service to vacationing Easterners as well as to the settlers of the lake region.

High with purpose, Captain Heerman returned to Reeds Landing, Minnesota, where his boat workshop was located, and there he drew plans for a boat that was one of the last he was ever to build. He named it the *Minnie-H* for his motherless little daughter.

He shipped the boiler and machinery and timbers for the *Minnie-H* by rail to Bartlett, Dakota Territory, end of the railway nearest Creel City, the first white community of the Devils Lake (city) area.

For thirteen days during the bitterest of winter weather, Heerman and his men struggled through drifted snow, hauling the boat parts to Creel City. The rudder, and several timbers were lost en route, so the Captain set up a saw mill and shaped native oak for the rudder and missing timbers.

The *Minnie-H* was ready for its first sailing on July 4, 1883. A sturdy vessel, it measured 110 feet in length, 20 feet across, and it drew 3½ feet of water. A gleaming white lady of the lake, she met the first regularly-scheduled train to arrive in the brand-new town of Devils Lake. All decked with flags, banners and bunting, and bearing aboard 500 cheering passengers, the "Minnie-H" sailed to Fort Totten, the army post across the lake.

And for sixteen Independence Days thereafter, folks in the lake region celebrated the day in the same manner.

Rails were laid on the wharf at Devils Lake to accommodate the freight and passengers going to Fort Totten, Minnewaukan and other points on the lake. Every summer hundreds of tourists boarded the *Minnie-H* for sight-seeing cruises over the "spirit waters" of local Indian legend. During Chautauqua season, the boat made daily excursions from Creel's Bay (which became the third largest Chautauqua center in the nation) to the beauty spots of Devils Lake.

Then in 1888, the fish suddenly disappeared from Devils Lake. The tragic fact was evident that the lake was shrinking. By 1909, the water had receded four miles from the city of Devils Lake, six miles from Minnewaukan, and more than two miles from Fort Totten. Although Captain Heerman made her ready for service that spring of 1909, the *Minnie-H* did not leave her boatyard. As the years passed, the lake's shrinkage was so great that the proud boat soon rested on dry ground.

Realizing that his days as a skipper were done, Edward

Heerman turned his attention to farming. He removed the pilot house from his boat, and made it into a playhouse for his grandchildren.

He salvaged the rudder of native oak, and declared he would present a gavel made from it to the first native-born governor of North Dakota. George Shafer was the first to qualify, and received the gavel during his term of office.

Edward Heerman was only sixteen when he began boating on the Mississippi, and at nineteen was in full charge of a side-wheel steamer on the Father of Waters. To the end of his 95 years, there remained in his heart the love of doing business upon the waters. Death came to the captain at Devils Lake in 1929.

33 The Golden-Haired Reverend Goldie

ONE of the most picturesque figures of early days in Pembina County was a missionary who wore his hair long and dyed it a bright canary yellow. The Reverend Oliver Goldie was Scotch, and a cousin of Robert Burns. He belonged to no particular denomination and had no certain dwelling. For twenty years he traveled from house to house in the northeastern corner of the state, preaching the Gospel.

He was a man said to be "wonderfully good," a man exceedingly gentle and tender of heart. Sometimes he would remain at a home only long enough to read the Bible and pray with the family; at other times, he elected to live for months with valued friends.

In his younger years, he had lived with the Indians, serving them as a missionary. He had acquired a few of their habits of living, also an Indian pony which he called "Billy Button" and cherished as one might a dear relative.

This horse was the old missionary's faithful companion for many years. The bond between the two was so close that Reverend Goldie frequently voiced the wish that his pony be buried beside him. But Billy Button died five years before his master — who managed to obtain an unwanted cemetery lot for him.

Reverend Oliver Goldie's burial place is near that of the "Martyrs of St. Joe" in the Walhalla Cemetery.

34 *Battling Country Lawyer*

COUNTY Attorney Grimson looked unbelievingly at the heartsick family seated in his Langdon office. For a moment he sat stunned, then exclaimed, "It doesn't seem possible that such a thing could happen here in America!"

But on the desk before him lay letters bearing strong evidence that early that year of 1922 his neighbor's son had been flogged to death in a Florida lumber camp. And there about him sat the slain boy's parents and his brothers, begging that justice be done.

Ben Tabert beseeched Grimson, "Will you help us?"

Grimson, the obscure country lawyer, turned to his farmer friend: "Yes, Ben, I will help you."

Gudmundur Grimson made good that promise. When, one year later, he had finished the Martin Tabert investigation, Grimson's name was known all over America. And to the New York *World* which rallied to his support in the case, was awarded the 1923 Pulitzer Prize for its public service in giving needful publicity to the investigation.

The tragic story of Martin Tabert which Grimson gradually jig-sawed together shocked the nation. It aroused such wrathful indignation among his fellow North Dakotans that they promptly subscribed $4000 to help finance the prosecution.

In the summer of 1921, Martin, a Munich, North Dakota farm boy of 22 years, eagerly set out to see America. He was confident he could pay his way, working as a laborer. He had never been outside Cavalier County when he left the Tabert farm.

Eventually, he reached Florida, where he found employment difficult to obtain because so much Negro labor was available. Broke, he got on a freight train to leave, but was discovered and taken to jail. Brought before a Leon County judge, he was sentenced to pay a fine of $25 and costs or spend three months in jail.

Martin wired his father: "IN TROUBLE AND NEED FIFTY DOLLARS TO PAY FINE FOR VAGRANCY. PLEASE WIRE MONEY IN CARE SHERIFF."

The Tabert family at Munich promptly sent a $75 bank draft to the sheriff at Talahassee. But the letter containing the money was returned by Sheriff J. R. Jones who noted on the envelope, "Party gone."

By this time the unsuspecting North Dakota youth had become the victim of a heinous system of slave labor — having the approval of law in a number of Florida counties. For each "convict" that Sheriff Jones could turn over to the Putnam Lumber Company for leased labor, he received a fee of $20. So Jones was disappointed when a man found guilty of vagrancy had funds — or could obtain them — to pay his fine. This fact accounted for the return of the letter containing the money for Martin Tabert.

Martin was delivered under lease to the Putman Lumber Company to work for three months in the swamps at building a railroad bed. Here, along with other men (obtained as he had been), he came under the immediate supervision of a brute known as "Captain" Walter Higginbotham. This Simon Legree urged his slaves to extreme effort by means of "Black Aunty" — a rawhide strap 5 feet long, 3-ply at the handle, tapering to a single ply at the end, and weighing 7½ pounds.

Martin was in good health when he arrived at the lumber camp. He was soon made ill by the gruelling labor, the unsanitary conditions of the camp, and the inhuman lashings with Black Aunty. He often worked waist-deep in poisonous swamp water. His feet became swollen with boils. His diet was field peas, corn bread and a little side pork.

The first time he was too sick with a fever to work, he begged Higginbotham to release him for the day. The whipping boss answered by seizing his whip. Martin dropped to his knees before the fiend and implored his mercy. But Black Aunty whistled through the air. She beat him down then, cut into his back as he lay on the muddy ground.

Martin dragged off to his work as Higginbotham, snarling in fury, lashed another man whose offense had been to look with reproach on the whipping boss.

One night after being charged with loafing on his job, Martin was called into the presence of 85 fellow "convicts" and ordered to lie down. The whipping boss was going to make an example of him to any prospective "loafers."

Higginbotham took a firm stance, uncoiled his murderous whip, and began to lash Martin's unprotected back. Florida law at that time limited the flogging of penal prisoners to ten lashes. But the terrified onlookers counted the times that Black Aunty seared the bloodied back, and the number was forty.

The tortured youth writhed and screamed so in his agony that the whipping boss placed his foot on his victim's neck to keep him still.

"O Lord!" Martin Tabert prayed, "Have mercy on me!"

"Don't call on the Lord," Higginbotham sneered, "call on *me;* I'm doin' this whippin'." His rage renewed, he lashed again . . . again . . . and again.

Then the boy was helped by his mates back to his vermin-infested bunk. The next morning, Saturday, he was flogged again before he crawled onto the flat car to go back to work. Sunday morning he was blind with fever. His bunk-mate, Glen Thompson, fed the delirious boy as best he could. On Monday, the physician hired by the Putman Lumber Company to "care" for their laborers, examined the half-conscious fellow, then gave Glen some quinine to administer to him. On Wednesday evening, the helpless, pitying men watched Martin Tabert — lacerated and gory on his verminous bed — breathe his last.

This much Gudmundur Grimson acquired in sworn statements sent to him by men who had been at the Putman Lumber Company with Martin Tabert. For more evidence, the Langdon lawyer went to Florida in January, 1923, and in the swamps and backwoods where the Munich boy had suffered and died, he hunted up eye-witnesses and obtained their sworn statements. Thoroughly prepared, he faced Sheriff J. R. Jones in his office, and began asking him some straight questions. The guilty man slammed shut his roll-top desk and quit the place.

His portfolio bulging with evidence, Gudmundur Grimson went to Governor Hardee of Florida, and secured the chief executive's promise of Grand Jury action on the Martin Tabert case. Confident that justice would be forthcoming, Grimson returned to North Dakota.

The Florida Grand Jury met, but took no action. So Mr. B. E. Groom, then of Langdon, laid the case before the North Dakota legislature. Immediately, the indignant North Dakota legislators passed a resolution calling on the State of Florida to conduct an investigation. It was the first time that one State had made such a request of another State.

Florida, experiencing a boom at the time, greatly resented the resolution. Its newspapers scathingly denounced the impertinence of the North Dakota farmer legislators and advised that they "go back home and slop their hogs." The Governor of Florida was pained; he feared the North Dakota legislative action would "improperly advertise our state." The only additional action taken was the arrest of Higginbotham.

Grimson realized that it would take considerable funds to continue the legal battle that would bring the whipping boss and his employers into deserved prosecution. He recalled that certain great newspapers sometimes had financed and reported investigations of merit. Accordingly, he wired ten of the largest dailies, appealing for their support. The New York *World* was first to respond.

Grimson returned to Florida, and quickly discovered that he was definitely unpopular in that state. Most Florida citizens were entirely unaware of the inhuman system of leasing prisoners to private enterprises to be treated like slaves, and they stoutly resented this upstart "Yankee" who meant to bring nation-wide disapproval and harmful publicity to their state. The accusation was made that Grimson was actually a tool hired by Californians. One Florida newspaper denounced the Langdon lawyer because this "ill-bred Northerner" addressed a Negro as "Mister."

Grimson, his swelling portfolio under his arm, went on his way, ignoring the vilification that fell his lot. In time, Samuel D. McCoy of the New York *World* came to accompany him at all times, and to report daily to his paper. Shortly, reporters from other great dailies were assigned to the case.

Embarrassed by the nation-wide publicity, the Florida legislature convened in April, 1923, gave immediate consideration to the North Dakota resolution and appointed a committee with intent to disprove the North Dakota charges. After producing witnesses and presenting his mass evidence to the Florida Grand Jury which then indicted Higginbotham, Grimson went to Tallahassee and appeared before the joint legislative committee. As the news spread over America, more and more evidence poured in from men who had known the horror of enforced labor in Florida and who now dared to speak out.

The legislative committee held hearings for thirty days. It was a memorable experience for Grimson the day the Florida committee chairman admitted the North Dakota charges and publicly thanked the battling country lawyer and his state for their "interference" in Florida affairs. Higginbotham was sentenced to 20 years in prison — but was later acquitted after a re-trial in Dixie County where the Putnam Lumber Company held 75 percent of the land.

Grimson then, on behalf of the Tabert family, prepared to bring suit against the Putnam Lumber Company. Settlement, however, was made without litigation, and the Company awarded $20,000 to Martin's family. Out of this amount, Grimson, in compliance with the family's wish, paid all the expenses incurred by the investigation and refunded all donations to the donors that could be traced. The substantial balance was turned over to the Taberts.

The miscarriage of justice, in the acquittal of Higginbotham, drew fire from newspapers all over the nation, and furthered interest in the case. The end product of Grimson's courageous investigation was a reform of prison laws in many parts of the United States. Hundreds of newspapers lauded the fearless country attorney. Said one, the Indianapolis *News*: "Gudmundur Grimson, a plain, ordinary prosecuting attorney, has found it within his power to start a reform of great significance, hundreds of miles from where he lived. America could stand a few more Gudmundur Grimsons."

The youngest of thirteen children, Gudmundur was born in Iceland on November 20, 1878. His family emigrated to America when he was a child, and settled on a homestead four miles north of Milton.

Nine years old, unable to speak English, Gudmundur started school in a sod-roofed, clay-chinked log schoolhouse. A few years later, he started walking the four miles to the Milton village school — then was denied admittance when the Milton school board ruled not to admit pupils from other districts. But the principal, John C. Nugent, interceded for the boy, got permission to fix for Gudmundur a special seat and assured the board the boy would be no expense to the Milton district.

Completing the eighth grade in 1895, Gudmundur procured a teacher's certificate, and taught country school at $30 a month for three years. With $150 saved, he thereupon enrolled in the preparatory course at the University of North Dakota. Knowing that his continued study would require frugal living, he moved into a small rough board shack across the railroad tracks from the University. Here, together with two other Icelandic youths, Vilhjalmur Stefansson and John G. Johnson, Gudmundur did some very light housekeeping. Their weekly budget for food totaled $1.60. Mostly, they ate Grapenuts — then highly advertised to be surpassingly nourishing. To accelerate their energies on frigid mornings, they drank hot Postum.

Keeping warm in that shanty was a major problem. The source of heat was a 4-lid cook stove whose firebox had to be replenished with wood every two hours — night as well as day. The boys took turns stoking that stove through the night. While they were at school during the day, the shanty would get so cold that foodstuffs froze.

The second year at school, the boys abandoned the shanty. Gudmundur got a job as janitor at Budge Hall, and also earned a little extra, carrying mail sacks. His third year, he was appointed University postmaster; at the little post office, part of his duties was also to handle sale of college texts books — and the ambitious Gudmundur, with the assistance of young Fred J. Traynor, developed the book selling until they had a thriving book store. The net result for the Milton youth was that when he had earned his Master's degree, he not only had all his school expenses paid, but had a cash balance of $750 besides.

Granted a fellowship in political economy, Grimson — the summer of 1905 — went to Chicago University where he studied for three terms. He returned to Grand Forks for the spring term at the University, completed his law course, and was granted the L.L.B. degree.

The following September he married, and a short while later hung out his lawyer's shingle at Munich — and there learned to know the Tabert family. Elected state's attorney in 1910, he moved to Langdon. After serving as county attorney for fourteen years, he was appointed Judge of the District Court of the Second North Dakota Judicial District. In five succeeding elections, he held the position without opposition.

Judge Gudmundur Grimson

North Dakota Historical Society photo

T. W. Thordarson

In 1949, he was appointed a judge of the North Dakota Supreme Court.

The battling county attorney of Cavalier County has won many honors. At the time of Iceland's Millenial Celebration, the University of Iceland conferred upon Grimson an honorary Doctor of Laws degree. Nine years later, the land of his birth made him a Grand Commander of the Order of the Falcon. For a month in 1949 — together with the world-renowned Arctic explorer, Dr. Vilhjalmur Stefansson who once shared with him the rigors of shanty life — Grimson was a guest of the Icelandic Government.

In 1932, accompanied by his wife, Grimson, as a representative of the Trans-American and Pan-American Air Lines, went to Europe and secured air-flight franchise from Iceland, and a similar contract from Denmark for air-bases in Greenland.

At the 1939 commencement exercises at the University of North Dakota, he was given a second Doctor of Laws degree, for the boy who so often supped on Grapenuts in the shanty across the tracks is today recognized as one of North Dakota's greatest jurists.

35 *Correspondence Study Crusader*

THE bitterness of frustration tinged the farmer's words as he lamented before his friend, "I got three kids — they're bright, and they're ambitious. They want to go on to high school, and Ma and me want them to — but with crop failures one year after another, we just can't afford it." Wistfully, he added, "If only we lived closer to a high school town!"

The friend nodded in thoughtful agreement. He well knew that living too far from a high school town, as well as financial lack, prevented hundreds of young people from continuing their schooling.

The farmer looked helplessly out across his parched fields. "Something ought to be done about it, Thordarson!" he said.

T. W. Thordarson went back to his desk at the North Dakota Agricultural College and resolved that something *would* "be done about it." All North Dakota farm children deserved opportunity for a high school education, no matter how far they might live from a high school town, no matter in what straits their parents might find themselves. And there were the many shut-ins who yearned for training that would broaden their horizon, perhaps be the way to security and the privilege of being self-supporting.

As Professor of Extension Education, Thordarson that year of 1933 directed the correspondence study of about 800 adults enrolled in courses in practical agriculture, and he also supervised evening classes at the College. He reflected how — as a farm lad able to attend common school only briefly in the fall and spring — he had studied at home during winter months to prepare for the eighth grade state examinations, and later, his first year as a teacher, had earned 12 quarter hours of college credit by correspondence study.

Convinced that for hundreds of rural youth, correspondence study could unbar the doors to high school education, Professor Thordarson plunged into a private study of correspondence study systems. He learned that in the western provinces of Canada, children in sparsely-settled areas were getting both common school and high school education by mail, that Australia and New Zealand employed similar methods for children in isolated homes, that a large high school at Benton Harbor, Michigan had operating — aside from the regular curriculum of classrooms subjects — a program of 300 correspondence courses enabling students to pursue special lines of study. Surely then, he deduced, in North Dakota where more than 40 percent of the rural youth were unable to attend a high school, a high school correspondence study system would serve to equalize educational opportunities.

Then one day in the fall of 1934, Thordarson read something in a newspaper which brought him to quick action. At a state convention of the Farmers Union, the item reported, a farm woman, Mrs. Lulu Evanson, had made a motion from the floor urging the organization to use its influence in getting state colleges to increase the number of high school correspondence courses offered. Such courses, she pointed out, would provide some high school training to eighth grade graduates even though they were unable to attend a regular high school.

Thordarson immediately wrote Farmers Union headquarters at Jamestown, outlining his plan for high school correspondence study. The following day two officials from the Jamestown office came to discuss the plan with him. They urged him to write a bill that would inaugurate such a study program. If he would do this, the Farmers Union would sponsor the bill at the next session of the legislature.

The bill became law in 1935. Professor Thordarson was appointed state director of the new venture. He and his staff had twenty courses ready when the school year began. To his amazement, 2087 enrollments poured in upon the seven teachers working in a basement room of Old Main. The second year, the number of subject enrollments was 4,569.

Some of the students enrolled were eighth grade graduates who returned to the rural schools to study high school subjects under the direct supervision of the local rural teacher. Regularly-enrolled high school students began enriching their own curriculum with correspondence courses that their own teaching staff could not provide. Shut-ins, farmers, village businessmen, and housewives availed themselves of this opportunity to study high school subjects. For some of them, it was the first opportunity to work for a high school diploma.

Thordarson himself proudly points to his Bachelor of Law diploma and a State Supreme Court certificate admitting him to the practice of law — the result of correspondence study.

At the present time (1954) the Supervised Study Center is located in Science Hall on the NDAC campus. A staff of

30 teachers gives instruction in more than 125 subjects. Each year there are between 6000 and 7000 subject enrollments received from approximately 3000 individual students.

The Center has developed, without legislative appropriations, a self-supporting 6000-volume rental book library, a collection of nearly 2500 educational films, 500 music and speech records, 1000 tape recordings available to schools and communities in the state, and also a Lyceum entertainment service.

North Dakota was the first state in the Union to inaugurate a legislated program of supervised correspondence study. There are now nearly 25 states which have adopted such a program.

The man chiefly responsible for this boon to rural youngsters, to shut-ins, and to the underprivileged, fought hard for his own education. Born on a homestead near Gardar in Pembina County, Theodore Waldemar Thordarson was eight years old when he first started school in a little one-room school two miles from his home.

He was scarcely able to make himself understood in the English language, but he was able to read and write Icelandic when he presented himself as a first grade pupil to the teacher, Joe Bjornson. He was already familiar — in the Icelandic — with such books as the Bible, *Quo Vadis, Ivanhoe, Oliver Twist*, some of Shakespeare's plays, the old Norse sagas, some Icelandic folklore and poetry.

For in the Icelandic immigrant's home, the family library was second in importance only to food for the body. The second year after the Icelanders had settled their colony on the Park and Tongue rivers, they had organized community cooperative libraries. In the Thordarson home, literature was discussed as readily and naturally as was livestock or farm crops. During the long winter evenings, Mother Thordarson would read aloud to her family from the old classics or chant the Icelander "rimur."

Three months in the fall, and three in the spring, was the maximum length of school term when Ted began his elementary education. Even this length was abbreviated after he reached ten and could manage a plow. By the time he was ready for the eighth grade, his interest in farm life was greatly reduced after a month's stint on a bundle team. This strenuous work with the threshing crew began at 4 a.m. and seldom ended until 10 p.m. The only temporary respite was provided by a good soaking rain, and the youth concluded that permanent respite from farm drudgery could come only by way of a high school education.

During the winter months, he studied at home in order to pass the state examinations, the completion of which would qualify him for high school entrance. After 27 months of common school attendance, 14-year-old Ted went to Valley City along with his older sister Solveig who was then in her Senior year at the Normal school there. The following year, with a younger sister, he did light housekeeping and attended school at Park River. When he was 17, his father (an invalid for 5 years) died, and further schooling must come largely by Ted's own earnings. Pitching bundles supplied him with the income which enabled him to graduate, two years later, from the Valley City Normal School.

He secured the position of high school principal at Wales, North Dakota. Desiring a college degree, he studied by correspondence and pinched his pennies. To help him acquire the coveted sheepskin, Thordarson at the end of the school year invested his total savings of $200 in a motorcycle. For having secured a sales contract with a nursery company, the young pedagog set forth, at 60 miles a gallon. In one pocket he had a brightly-illustrated catalog of lovely flowers and magnificient shade trees; in another, an order book.

From dawn until dark he would call on farmers and small town folks who were weary of barren prairie yards and eager to hear this prophet of windbreaks and landscaped beauty. By the end of his first day, Thordarson's commission on sales netted him a larger income than he had ever earned in a week's time. His expenses were trimmed to a minimum for farm folks invited him to meals or to spend the night. In one month's time he had secured enough funds to finance the college year ahead.

He returned to the Gardar farm to help with harvesting and threshing, and to take Gardar Township girls for a breezy ride on the luggage carrier of his motorcycle. He was the envy of neighborhood boys who considered him a veritable speed demon as he raced over the dirt roads and cavorted down cow trails in the open pastures.

And so, by the grace of his motorcycle, Thordarson attained his B. S. and M. S. degrees at the North Dakota Agricultural College. Then he took a full-time job with the nursery company, working as a landscape architect.

Their pioneering years behind them, young towns in North Dakota and Montana were awakening to municipal pride and welcomed this nursery man who could both plan and sell them the plantings for prairie town parks. Prosperous business men delighted in the service of this Landscape Architect who, on paper, bedecked their elegant new homes with appropriate verdure.

Only a year later, the Landscape Architect arrived at Fort Snelling — a bewildered candidate for officer's training. Undecided which field of army service he would enter, he determined to seek the counsel of an officer.

At the Fort gates, he met a man in uniform and asked him where he might find an officer. The soldier pointed toward a Major standing not far distant.

Timidly, the Landscape Architect approached the Army brass, and began a recital of his educational background. The biographic account was quickly interrupted with, "Follow that path — it will take you to your barracks." The barracks happened to be of the Field Artillery, and thus it was that the Landscape Architect made his decision as to which branch of service he should enter.

He began his "Ninety-Day Wonder" training. Half of the candidates were discharged before the period was over. The

Landscape Architect from North Dakota was one of those who survived the rigors of the training; he earned a commission as lieutenant because: "I could ride any old farm plug, pick up a horse's hind leg and clean the hoof without any apparent fear, and I could drive horses without getting excited — and there was plenty of excitement when a whole battery was in action with six horses at each gun, and a hundred horses and some 150 candidates clopping down the parade grounds."

On becoming a lieutenant, Ted Thordarson was as exultant as when he got his motorcycle. Fairly scintillating confidence, he — on his first leave — returned to Gardar Township and there married a neighbor girl, Kathryn Olafson.

After two years of training troops, he was discharged in 1919 at Camp Funston, Kansas and in that state resumed civilian life as County Extension Agent in Barton County.

His first duty as county agent was to demonstrate blackleg vaccination. He had never seen such a demonstration, so, thoughtfuly and fearfully — he prepared himself by reading instructions in a veterinary pamphlet. Then he stepped before a crowd of experienced cattle men, filled a syringe with serum and stuck the needle through the hide of a bawling calf. The men went home convinced that they had a new county agent who was well qualified to help them with their livestock health problems.

Among his most memorable experiences as county agent was the handling of a harvest labor problem. A year after the War, the railroads were still being operated by the Government, and transients were not allowed to ride freight trains. In Barton County there was a bumper crop of wheat; 5000 transient laborers were needed to help harvest it — and due to the passenger fare only a trickle of workers came. Thordarson saw one of them get up on a rain barrel and auction himself off for $12 a day, before a crowd of waiting farmers.

Thordarson raised funds from Barton County business men to pay train fare of laborers to their county, then went to Kansas City. After much difficulty, he obtained laborers and two railway coaches to carry them. He started back with them at night, and wherever the train stopped, a crowd of distraught farmers would try to bribe Thordarson's men into their own service, urging them to come through the windows of the coaches. Only a few of the laborers, however, deserted.

When further such excursions failed to bring sufficient help, Barton County townspeople closed their shops and went out to help their farm neighbors harvest the record crop.

One day Thordarson received a wire requesting him to meet with an official of Montgomery Ward & Company. As a result, he was hired as agricultural consultant for that firm. Later, he became advertising and sales promotion manager for the St. Paul branch and supervised the publication of the mail order catalogs.

He remained with Montgomery Ward & Company until post-war depression years, worked for a time as a colonization promoter for the Northern Pacific railway, then returned to his *alma mater* to direct the training of World War veterans.

In 1925, the NDAC alumni association offered the position of half-time secretary to Thordarson. He accepted after the College agreed to give him opportunity to develop correspondence study in practical agriculture courses. He combined the two jobs until both fields of work developed sufficiently to require full-time directors. He stayed with the College extension office until 1935, when he became state director of the Division of Supervised Study.

Today there are thousands of North Dakota citizens who have a high school education because this farm son did not forget (once his own struggles for an education were ended) those who yearned for further schooling. And many there are who have entered upon careers which would have been closed to them had this man failed to remember with compassion, that "the hungry sheep look up and are not fed."

36 Prairie-Town Merchant

"MICHIGAN! Michigan! This way out!"
The backwoods youth in home-made garb clutched his cardboard-and-canvas telescope suitcase, and in hopeful excitement, stepped off Train No. 9.

From the railway station that April day of 1907, Manville Johnson surveyed his commercial mecca of Michigan, North Dakota. Across the muddy street was a livery stable, a two-story brick hotel, a blacksmith shop and a tapering fringe of lesser buildings out toward the open prairie. Where, he wondered, was the Michigan Mercantile Company store where he, graduate of a correspondence course in accounting, had been promised a position as bookkeeper?

It was noon, and he was hungry. He decided to eat before finding the store. After making safe passage across the street — on planks bridging the biggest puddles — he went to the hotel and made his self-conscious way to the dining room.

He was shown to a table and took a seat, unaware that he was at the "Head Table." Here — because there were napkins and a bowl of oranges — the dinner would cost 50 cents; the same food would have cost 35 cents at any other table.

From across the Head Table a sophisticated traveling salesman surveyed the awkward eighteen-year-old from Minnesota with open amusement. And Manville Johnson — destined to become the head of a chain of stores — blushed selfconsciously, felt his own awkwardness increase as the meal progressed.

Once he had eaten, he quickly left the table, and located the Michigan Mercantile Store a block away. With thudding heart, he sought the manager who greeted him briefly, appraised him coolly, and then, without giving any instructions as to his employment, left him standing in the middle of the store.

A few of the sales clerks were friendly, however, and chatted with him occasionally as the afternoon wore on. Manville learned from them that his arrival had been anticipated — for one reason: he was the nephew of Marcus Johnson of St. Paul, the political potentate, the friend of governors and presidents, the wealthy co-owner of properties such as the Michigan Mercantile Company.

It was near supper time when the store manager came inviting Manville to accompany him home for the evening meal. This hospitality gesture was out of deference to the uncle, and it was also to cushion the backwoods nephew for the news that Louise, niece of the store manager, had already been made bookkeeper at the store; for Manville the job of store flunky awaited. His salary would be $10 a month plus board and room. His place of board and room would be the home of a Michigan Mercantile Company customer who had a long overdue account at the store.

Next morning the supplanted bookkeeper was shown a broom, the barrel of sweeping compound, and a supply of dust rags. He was not long in learning that he would be closely associated with the broom, the sweeping compound and the dust rags for the town's streets were of a rich, loamy soil that turned to dust in dry weather and became adhesive after every shower.

Michigan Mercantile store hours followed no fixed schedule. Some clerks were on hand as early as seven in the morning. The place remained open to suit the convenience of the customer — usually closing at 10 in the evening. On Saturday night, when most of the farmers were in town, it stayed open until midnight. And there was need of the store flunky every hour of the day.

Another of Manville's regular duties was the hauling of freight from the depot every afternoon. Through the day there were deliveries to customers in town.

Then there was the prune renovation.

A bargain purchase of a hundred 100-pound sacks of prunes had been stored in the damp basement, and only a small portion of them had been sold. The prunes were spoiling — some "sugaring," others rotting. Many of the burlap sacks contained great lumps of the fruit pressed together in a state of decay.

But there was at hand a prune-renovating machine consisting of a large metal vat in which was suspended a perforated drum. The new store flunky was told how to use this ingenious device for the resuscitation of the prunes.

Thereupon Manville poured the vat half full of water. Then he dumped the sugared and slightly damaged prunes he had sorted from the spoiled ones into the drum. Next he set to work revolving the drum of prunes, and thus the prunes — churned in the water — lost their sugar coating.

This prune laundering, however, also removed the sweet taste and natural gloss of the fruit. So there was need for a second churning, this time in a 50-50 solution of water and molasses.

For a final touch of renovation, the wet prunes were carried to the second floor and spread out thinly. Once or twice a day, Manville stirred the lot with a garden rake. The upstairs being rather "open," the elixir of North Dakota air soon revived the prunes to respectable presentation in the grocery department, where they were priced at 6 pounds for a quarter.

In that pre-Pure Foods Laws era, the store flunky had yet another job, one which furnished him with even more regular employment than that of prune renovation. This was the packing of butter.

Farmers then packed butter in jars that contained from 5 to 20 pounds. The peak of butter production was during the summer. Transportation of butter from farm to town was by slow team and wagon. Farmers living far from a marketing center came at rare intervals, their wagon or buggy floors covered with butter jars.

After a long jaunt over the prairie trails, under the hot sun, the butter which reached Michigan was as soft as pancake batter. To the flunky fell the job of packing this butter in 300-pound wooden barrels. These barrels had been soaked in water in order to tighten the staves. The bulk of the butter purchased from the farmers was taken to the cool basement, the rest of it left in the warm store. In the early morning, Manville would dump the firm butter into the barrel, then pour the soft over it, to fill in the spaces. He finished the job by use of a large butter stomper.

Once a week a refrigerated car, sent through on the local freight, transported the Michigan butter to a creamery at Alexandria, Minnesota.

It chanced one midsummer day that this train was late, extra late. For hours, the huge casks of butter had stood in the open sun on the depot platform. When, at last, the train arrived, the brakemen — rushing to make up lost time — attacked the first butter cask too recklessly. Since the liquid butter had by this time oozed between the barrel's staves, the cask slipped from the trainmen's hold. It fell to the ground and exploded, drenching the train crew with oily, rancid butter.

Occasionally during his long day, the store flunky might be called to help serve customers — usually in the grocery department. Here he learned that the sale and distribution of butter, even when fresh and sweet, had its involvements.

For there existed in that day and place, the buttermakers' caste.

Mrs. Olson, an excellent housekeeper, made superior butter. Her butter reputation was such that when she came to town with her 5-pound jar of butter, Michigan housewives were on hand at the store to make sure of their share of her good butter. Mrs. Olson, on discovering that hers was the rarified atmosphere of Super Butter Maker, imperiously requested — and received — a premium price for her product.

Mrs. Pedersen made good butter, too. The Michigan housewives whose habit it was to taste butter before buying, came to agree that Mrs. Pedersen's butter was on a par with Mrs. Olson's. Soon Mrs. Pedersen, also, was getting a premium price for her output.

Mrs. Swenson, learning of Mrs. Olson and Mrs. Pedersen's standing, aspired to climb the butter ladder, likewise. But no amount of taste-testing could raise the quality of Mrs. Swenson's butter, and the clerks came to fear the wrath of a woman whose butter was scorned. A day of jubilee it was, for country store clerks, when creameries and uniform retail prices brought an end to the buttermakers' caste.

At times when sales were brisk, Johnson was elevated to counter work. But for a boy who aspired to an accounting career, selling groceries offered little incentive. Certain operational methods morally offended his sense of justice and often incensed him. In that day, merchandise prices were not fixed; many customers haggled over prices. A particular sales clerk at the Mercantile store had a reputation for drastic price-cutting, and naturally customers preferred his services. Favored customers always expected special concessions. The store's cash-and-carry customers paid full price on their purchases, while many charge customers received a 10 per cent discount when finally they paid their bills.

Manville observed, but was powerless to correct, phases of poor management that resulted in financial loss to the store, and practices which did nothing to build good will among the customers. The flunky tasks were monotonous, and his enforced shabbiness disheartened him. His $10 wage did not permit him to purchase a more suitable wardrobe — and on the streets of Michigan, a popular ditty was frequently sung as a taunt to him:

Oh where did you get that hat?
And where did you get that tie?

What glamour his famous Uncle Marcus had found in the merchandising world was something Manville could not discern. One thing was certain to him: he wanted schooling that would enable him to enter upon a more satisfying career.

Knowing that store personnel would be cut to a minimum during the three slack months following Christmas, he decided to attend the Normal School at Mayville — where he had studied the previous winter.

At that time he had worked as janitor at the Mayville hospital, and with the help of his sister Annie living on a farm nearby he had managed well enough.

When he first entered the Normal School, he was not even an eighth grade graduate. With other January students in his plight, he was placed in a "B Class" of overgrown farm youths who needed "just plain reading, writing and arithmetic."

One of their teachers, a Miss Bentley, became so dismayed over their intellectual shortcomings that she asked "Wouldn't you *really* like to learn?" When Manville and his colleagues made no reply, she singled out John Swenson and inquired of him, "Would you rather be doing something else than studying, Mr. Swenson?"

"Oh ya," that son of the soil replied, "I think I rather be sitting on a gang plow."

Since Manville did not share John's ambition, he had persisted in his studies, and the following summer also attended the Normal School at Moorhead, Minnesota.

Now at Mayville for his second winter term, he was admitted to regular college courses. His self-assurance grew. When he returned to the store flunky job that spring, his work held more challenge.

One day he read in a trade magazine an article on store merchandising arrangement, and was led to make recommended changes in the grocery department. A representative from Reid, Murdock Company of Chicago was so pleased with Manville's display of Monarch products, he insisted on having a picture of it.

Since there was frequent turnover in store personnel, young Johnson was often requested to take over a partieular position until a replacement could be hired. Consequently, he gained more and more sales experience. Every once in a while, though, because a delivery boy had quit, he would be back hauling freight and packing butter — renovating the last of the bargain-priced prunes.

After three years in the store, he one day was approached by the manager and abruptly asked. "How would you like to manage a store of your own?"

It happened that a general store in the town had just closed out. Rumor had it that an outside firm planned to move in — that the Michigan Mercantile was due for some sharp competition.

The Mercantile Company, therefore, obtained the recently vacated building with the intent of launching a subsidiary enterprise. Manville Johnson eagerly accepted the offer made him, borrowed money for a one-third share in the new store — which was to bear the name of "M. A. Johnson Company."

The new manager unlocked the empty store building and found it was in great need of repair. Dirt and dust lay everywhere. Stale water, a foot deep, covered the basement floor.

He was cleaning the place when a high school girl noticed the unlocked door and walked in. Seeing the delivery boy from Michigan Mercantile busy with the broom, she asked, "What are you doing here?"

"I'm going to open a store."

"Honest true?"

"Yes, honest true."

"Who is going to run it?"

"I am."

"Huh! Yeah, that's good! Tell me, though, honest true, who *is* going to run it?"

The girl later found out — "honest true;" and yet later, she became one of M. A. Johnson's employees.

From the first the little store flourished. The new manager was full of ideas, and so eager to put them into practice that he almost begrudged the time spent in sleep. He introduced a 5-and-10 counter, and did special sales advertising. He steered away from traditional practices that he knew were unsound. As he formulated his Company policies, he kept in mind his own big goal: to have customers say of his store, "We like to trade there."

In 1913, Uncle Marcus arrived in town to attend the annual conference of stockholders. The "little store," it was found, had done so well that Manville Johnson was promoted to the managership of both the Michigan stores.

During the next decade, the young merchant worked early and late to make his business successful. In the interest of self-improvement, he took a two-year business administration course by correspondence from La Salle University, and he also studied public speaking with a Michigan lawyer, Elwood Fitchette.

Prosperity followed World War I, but the lush years ended with a sudden financial crash. Many people were predicting that automobile transportation spelled doom to the small prairie town for retail trade would go to the cities and the larger towns.

Manville Johnson determined not to join the stampede to the city, but to keep his business where, and as, it was: a country store. Through the tight-fisted years of the 20s, he inaugurated policies that were to develop his enterprise from that first store at Michigan to the present (1954) chain of fourteen stores. More than 200 townspeople and farmers now are profit-sharing partners in the Johnson Home Town Stores Company.

It was years ago, when he was a boy of ten, that Johnson entered on his first commercial enterprise. This was the soliciting and delivering of laundry for his mother at lumber camps in the vicinity of their Bear Creek cabin home. His knack for trading even then displayed itself. He found that in the camps fresh milk was a rarity, and that men obliged to eat beef-tallow oleomargarine fairly drooled at the mere mention of fresh butter.

The day the boy appeared at camp with a pail of fresh

milk and a small jar of butter, he found the camp cook eager to barter for this dairy manna. "What," asked the man, "would your mother like in exchange for the milk and butter?"

Young Manville eyed the great stores of dried fruit, bacon, sugar, flour, the assortment of condensed foods. He thought of the scant provisions in his own home, then tremulously pointed toward some dried fruit in a barrel near him. The cook emptied the milk pail and filled it to the top with the delicious dried apricots. The three years Manville carried laundry — and an offering of fresh milk and butter — to the camps, the generous lumberjack cooks always started him home with a happy step.

So began the commercial trading career of the man who today heads a most unique chain of small department stores — a chain totally without city ambitions, and dedicated to serving rural folks in their own community.

"M. A.," as the president of Johnson Home Town Stores has come to be known, has his headquarters at Larimore. Like most men who have attained success through hard and honest effort, he has no pretentious airs.

At odd times, he may be found in the warehouse, with his sleeves rolled up. Now and then he has been confronted by a representative of some manufacturing firm, or a traveling salesman, with the question, "Can you tell me where I can find Mr. Johnson?"

In his mild and unassuming manner, the company president has replied, "I am Mr. Johnson."

Again and again has come the retort: "But I want to talk to *the* Mr. Johnson."

37 Horatio Alger of the Prairies

EACH year the American Schools and Colleges Association presents ten Horatio Alger awards to men who have risen from poverty and obscurity to merited success. The youngest man ever to receive this honor is Harold Schafer of Bismarck.

Responsibility came early in Harold Schafer's life. He was fifteen years old, a Junior in high school, when his father died, leaving him to support his mother and younger sister.

In order to continue his education, and still help his family, Harold arranged with high school authorities at Bismarck so that he could take all his classes in the forenoon. This enabled him to work in a clothing store through the afternoons. In the evenings he had a job at a filling station.

By the time he had completed high school, Harold had decided he would be a farmer as his father had been. Wanting agricultural training, he enrolled at the North Dakota Agricultural College the fall of 1929.

Again there was a rigid work schedule in addition to classes. He was a sales clerk in a Fargo clothing store afternoons, a filling station attendant from 7 to 10 in the evening, then a restaurant dishwasher until 1 a.m. On the campus he managed to care for a sheep which brought him first prize at the Little International Fair; he also won the hog judging contest.

After a year at NDAC, Harold engaged in farming and found it anything but lucrative those drouth-plagued years. He went back to Bismarck and worked in a clothing store for five years.

M. A. Johnson

Harold Schafer

Harry F. McLean

Photo by courtesy of
W. H. Falconer,
Bismarck

Then in 1936, he became a traveling salesman for a paint and glass firm. As he rambled about southwestern North Dakota, he began to get ideas for a business of his own. So, in 1942, he invested in a few barrels of floor wax, packaged the wax in a rented store basement, then scurried about the state selling Gold Seal Floor Wax to stores.

He grossed $902.02 that first year. Discouragements, many problems faced the Gold Seal Company those early years, but Harold Schafer always applied a remedy which had become his personal motto: "Work."

By 1945 his Company had progressed so that his floor wax was selling well throughout North Dakota. He decided he would expand his sales territory into neighboring states, and picked his wife's home town of Aberdeen, South Dakota, for his first out-of-state try. With his partner, C. O. Bruer, he canvassed Aberdeen retail stores for an entire week without making a single sale.

But the week's failure made Schafer all the more determined to succeed. "I could just hear them saying, 'Boy that guy is a blowhard. I just wonder how much wax he really sells in North Dakota. He can't be much good or he would have sold some in Aberdeen. His product can't be much good, either, or it would have sold itself in Aberdeen. Too bad a nice girl like Marian got mixed up with this guy.'"

As he sat in his hotel room, desperately trying to think of some way to get Gold Seal floor wax introduced in the town, an idea came to him which was to become the formula for much of his success: *Perform something worthy to be remembered.*

Next morning, he was out calling before the stores had opened. He found his first prospect sweeping, so Harold grabbed the broom, and helped the man with his morning clean-up. When he walked out of that store, he had his first Aberdeen order for Gold Seal floor wax.

He came upon the second merchant perspiring as he unloaded a truckload of flour. For the next half hour, Schafer tossed flour sacks upon his own broad shoulders, and soon had another storekeeper willing to give Gold Seal a try.

He found a lumberyard man unenthusiastically surveying a couple hundred sacks of cement reposing on a truck. When the 6-foot Gold Seal salesman offered to help stack that cement in the warehouse, the lumber merchant considered him with cheerful appreciation. Harold Schafer was dusty and weary from cement toting when he sat down to write out the third order for Gold Seal floor wax.

At the next grocery store, he helped the proprietor wash shelves, and arrange the display of competitive merchandise. But when he left the store, he had the satisfaction of knowing that Gold Seal wax would also be on display there.

Aberdeen merchants were soon remembering this Gold Seal salesman, not for his sales talk as much as for his jovial helpfulness; in two days, 41 of the 44 independent retail stores were handling Schafer's product.

One day he heard a chewing gum jingle, and wondered if some easily-remembered rhyme might help Gold Seal sales. With this in mind, he contacted a New York advertising agency and was informed they did not handle accounts under $250,000 annually.

Schafer went to Minneapolis, obtained the services of an advertising agency there that would consider working with a prairie-town salesman. By late 1947, this agency went ahead with national advertising of Gold Seal products; sales shot up from $800,000 in 1947 to $8,500,000 in 1948.

The Gold Seal Company now spends $1,500,000 annually for promotional purposes. An estimated ten million housewives use its three major products. Headquarters are at Bismarck, and there are seven regional offices around the nation.

Schafer also sells Gold Seal products in nearly fifty foreign countries. Yet he neither invented nor makes the products his company sells. Seven million dollars is grossed annually buying the products from manufacturer, then packaging and selling.

As one enters the offices of the Gold Seal Company, one sees on the wall these words: "Great minds discuss ideas. Average minds discuss events. Small minds discuss people." A large mural portraying a pioneer wielding an axe depicts Harold Schafer's personal motto: "Work."

38 "Mister Give Away"

AT the head of the State Capitol grounds stands an impressive ten-foot monument. Sculptured by Avard Fairbanks, "The Pioneer Family" symbolizes progress and the spirit of the west. Dedicated in 1947, it honors the memory of the pioneers of the northwest.

The bronze statue — valued at $50,000 — was given to his native state by Harry F. McLean, a man whose generosity has earned him the nickname of "Mister Give Away."

One of the four sons of John McLean, the first elected mayor of Bismarck, Harry was born at 233 First Street. He served as a page in the North Dakota legislature, and was graduated from the Bismarck high school in 1902.

He took a job as water boy with a construction company then building the Linton branch of the Northern Pacific railway. Within a few months he was made commissary man, and continued to earn promotions. After taking time out for a year at a Fargo business college, he returned to work with the construction company and eventually became its head.

After going to Canada with his company, he became wealthy and internationally famous because of his achievements as a construction engineer. In the early 30s, he built the great Abitibi Dam about seventy miles north of Cochrane, Ontario. To accomplish this, McLean and his men deflected the course of the Abitibi River by means of a tunnel cut through solid rock. The concrete-lined tunnel was constructed during frigid winter months, the builders racing against the time of the spring thaws.

McLean accomplished what other experts declared impossible when he built the Flin Flon railway across frozen muskeg. While his men were dumping tons of ballast on the route across muskeg, the less visionary engineers shook their heads and prophesied that with the arrival of warm weather, ballast and rails would sink into the muskeg. But every summer since the railway was completed, the muskeg — insulated against thawing by the heavy roadbed — has remained solid, and trains rush across the "impossible" route.

Harry McLean and his men have built railway tunnels, bridges, yards; and laid tracks and ballast in both Canada and the United States. This former water boy's list of large-scale engineering feats includes several hydro-electric power developments, the building of military bases and wartime housing, the construction of docks, breakwaters, ocean terminals, and airports. One of his most outstanding achievements is a New York City water-supply concrete-lined tunnel 15 feet in diameter and nearly 6 miles in length — cut through rock and requiring nearly five years to complete.

Only close friends in his home state learned of these accomplishments. Most North Dakotans had never heard of Harry F. McLean until newspapers began carrying stories about "Mister Give Away," a mysterious philanthropist who went about giving away $100 bills "just to make people happy."

One of these stories related that a Halifax, Canada, cab driver was handed $240 in cash as advance pay for chauffering McLean on one of his give-away sprees. As they drove about the streets, McLean would spot a soldier or sailor, and order the driver to stop. Then "Mister Give Away" would step out and hand the dumbfounded service man a crisp green bill. When at length McLean decided to call it a day, he explained to his driver, "I like to help out people who have to work hard for a living." Then he handed the driver a check in the amount of $2000 — a special gift for the man's infant son.

Once in a Toronto hospital, "Mister Give Away" had a happy time passing out the green stuff to veterans and a number of employees there. At his hotel in that city he surprised the switchboard girl almost past speech when he gave her a thousand dollars to share with eight hotel bellboys.

So it was quite in character for the man to honor his home state with the gift of "The Pioneer Family" monument. But it is not the only memorial that Harry McLean has erected.

Representative of his compassion for the hard-working men who risk their lives in effecting his engineering miracles are the "Sons of Martha" monuments he rears upon completion of each major project. These memorials are of stone and bear a plaque engraved with Kipling's immortal poem.

Harry McLean is noted for his consuming desire to eliminate the dangers that threaten his workers. In addition to his requirements that all possible precautions be taken against hazards, his construction camps are outfitted with complete hospital equipment and personnel to care for any unpreventable injuries.

Perhaps the greatest reward falling to Harry McLean is the loyalty of his men — the trust they place in this man who believes that the ordinary laborer deserves as much credit as the man who does the planning and gives the orders.

39 Three-Facet Artist

SMALL boy Paul Broste kept his overall pockets so full of odd and colorful stones that the suspender buttons were always pulling off. Schoolboy Paul — on entrance day, at five years of age — wrote his name on the blackboard in such admirable script that the teacher would not erase it for several days.

Grades later he drew pictures in his tablet and was punished for using school time thus. But when it was a freehand map of the United States that he one day drew, the teacher proudly tacked it on the wall of the rural Pekin, North Dakota schoolroom. It was not removed until a day when the county superintendent of schools saw it and, claiming priority to the schoolboy's work, took it against the teacher's wishes to put on display at his office. Young Paul privately considered that the map's creator was the rightful one to possess it, but he reacted in character. "Let them scrap over it," he inwardly said, "I'll draw a better one next time."

Art was an inherent love in Paul Broste. From the first he wanted to acquire it, create it, and share it.

Grown to manhood, he — back in 1916 — took a homestead near Parshall, and there he still lives. During the first winters on the claim he worked joyously at drawing and painting; then, for three successive winters he attended the Chicago Art Institute — returning always in good time to get his grain crops sowed.

His farming prospered, and it expanded. Eventually, Broste had 1440 acres under cultivation. Success as a farmer, however, could not completely satisfy him; always there was in him the artist's desire for creating beauty. Whenever there was time to spare, he was busy with brush and palette. He

Paul Broste

View showing rocks and oil paintings in Broste museum, Parshall

The two sphere trees in the Broste museum

entered oil paintings at the Midwest Fair at Minot, and won many prizes. He was pressed to accept orders for scenes and portraits and other specified subjects. A few of his portrait assignments (that of Mrs. William H. Parker, mother of Lottie Parker of Minot; and of Elias Bjorlee, father of Dr. Ignatius Bjorlee — a friend and relative) Broste considers his best work.

Much as other people admired his paintings, the farmer-artist himself was not content with the quality of his canvases; he felt unable to achieve the ideals he set for himself as a painter. So he forsook his brush and palette, turned back to that interest which had impelled small boy Paul to jam his pockets with stones. Now and then, through the years, he had added rocks to his boyhood collection.

In 1940, on a trip through the Southern states, Broste found himself lured to places where rock specimens were sold. Here and there, he bought a few, stowed them in his car.

Home on the farm again, his stone collection took on new meaning. The beautiful colors and patterns in the rocks begged to be brought out, enhanced.

So Paul Broste engrossed himself in the making of rock spheres. By the tedious, laborious hand process he cut, ground, and polished 370 of them, varying in size from less than an inch to over a foot in diameter. Entirely without intending to do so, he became the possessor of the world's largest private rock collection.

He did not come to realize the extent nor the quality of his lapidary work until he attended a meeting of the American Federation of Mineralogical Societies, held in Milwaukee in the summer of 1950.

Considering himself as merely a dirt farmer from North Dakota seeking fellowship with august scholars, Paul Broste decided he had better bring with him some sort of credentials. So he and his nephew, Ronald Broste, welded together a strap iron "tree" in the branches of which 80 spheres were gracefully arranged.

He brought this unique tree, together with a hundred additional spheres, with him to Milwaukee, and to his great surprise, he was featured in the Milwaukee *Journal* and several other newspapers. Later, he was the subject of an article in the September, 1950 *Mineralogist Magazine.*

There are now two of the sphere trees in the museum room of bachelor Broste's home. In this special room are showcases displaying mineral specimens from all over the world — many of them in polished form. This open museum is consistent with the owner's love of sharing beauty as well as collecting and creating it. There are more than two thousand names signed in the visitor's register.

On the walls of this private museum hang a number of Broste's oil paintings — Missouri River landscapes and scenes, some striking portraits of Franklin Delano Roosevelt, of young Shirley Temple, of farm girls sitting upon a windswept North Dakota hill. Amazing as Broste's rock collection is, his talent as a painter impresses numbers of his visitors as being the greater.

Because visitors frequently express the wish that they might purchase some souvenir — even just a postcard view of the Broste museum — this farmer ventured upon a third facet of art, the writing of poetry. In 1953, he published a souvenir book entitled *A Proem* which contains numerous photographs of his rocks, of his paintings, and which also includes original poems expressing the philosophy of this farmer-artist.

The years ahead will see more and more folks driving seven and a half miles south and west of Parshall to a farm home where one man, driven by an insatiable hunger for creating beauty, has made for himself and for others a prairie artist's citadel.

40 *Gold Star Bandmaster*

ON Memorial Day, 1870, folks at Barre, Vermont watched the 8th Regiment Vermont Volunteers Band parading down their streets — its drummer an eleven-year old boy whacking away at a big bass drum carried by a larger boy. The sight of the too-small drummer did not amuse the Barre folks, but brought back memories of the band director who had died in Sherman's March to the Sea.

The young drummer boy was that director's son. When the remaining members of George B. Putnam's band at last returned home and reorganized, it was his son Clarence they chose to be their drummer.

This was not Clarence's first experience with music groups. As he long afterward remarked, "I took up music when I was two years old. At that time, my mother who sang in our church choir at Barre, would lay me behind the organ, and I sang in that choir as long as I lived in Barre."

His mother was his first music teacher; she had him reading and singing the alto part in choir music by the time he was six years old. He was nine when he played his first band engagement. At ten, he was singing in a production of Handel's "Messiah." By the time he was seventeen, Clarence was directing the band that once had followed his father's baton.

He elected music as his career, and went to Boston where he studied voice with Chadwick, harmony and directing under Zerahn. At Boston he appeared in a presentation of the Gilbert and Sullivan operetta "HMS Pinafore," and was understudy to a leading tenor.

Then his mother — herself a concert contralto — asked him to quit the study of music, and enter a medical school at Philadelphia. After one year there, he went to Chicago to study — playing in orchestras to help finance his education. He was graduated from the Hahnemann Medical College in 1883, an honor student in his class.

He practiced medicine at Moorhead, Minnesota for a year, then moved to Ada. After eight years his country practice proved too rigorous for his health — so Putnam went to Superior, Wisconsin, and there returned to his first love of music. He directed choirs, orchestras and bands, and taught voice and wind instruments. During the five years there he regained his health.

In 1896 he went to Chicago for postgraduate work in surgery, and afterward settled in Casselton, North Dakota to practice. Five years later he opened medical offices in the Edwards Building on Broadway in Fargo, and was just nicely established in his practice when fire destroyed his entire medical library and all his equipment — and this five days after his insurance had lapsed. At the time he had a wife, a mother and two children to support.

Three days after the fire, on January 10, 1904, the young physician turned teacher. Dr. Clarence S. Putnam hiked through the deep snow to the new brick building (now Old Main) which housed the recently-established North Dakota Agricultural College, and began teaching four classes in arithmetic.

Three months later, need of a temporary band leader arose. "Doc" took over the 16-piece band — and for the next forty-one years continued to swing his baton for that organization. When he died February 25, 1944, Putnam had developed NDAC's Gold Star Band into a 125-member group, had directed several municipal organizations (band, orchestra, choral, operatic), and had become one of the most unforgettable members of the College faculty.

Trim, precise, even in the final years of his service, Doc marched at the head of his military band as peppy as any collegian. Tardiness was something he could not tolerate. Once, because of muddy roads, part of his band straggled in after the opening whistle of a UND-NDAC basketball game

Dr. Clarence S. Putnam

at Grand Forks — and for a long time afterwards, Doc was embarrassed. To the end of his long NDAC career, he demonstrated a phenomenal ability to recall alumni who had played in his band. He could call them by name and even recollect an incident from each one's college days.

As he walked about the campus, students caught step with him, glad for a chance to chat with him. Often in the boys' dormitory or some classroom the amiable professor was surrounded by students who enjoyed drawing him into their discussions.

Clarence Putnam composed the music for the North Dakota Hymn, wrote a North Dakota March, the NDAC Toast Song, and several band compositions. In recognition of his accomplishments, he was given the honorary commission of Lieutenant Colonel by Governor George F. Shafer. In 1930, the Blue Key organization at the College presented him with a Doctor of Service degree, and five years later he was the first North Dakotan admitted to the American Bandmasters' Association.

The 1935 Bison yearbook was dedicated to Doc. It quoted the philosophy of the much-loved, silver-haired man who walked with such sprightly step before his Gold Star Band:

Nobody grows old by merely living a number of years. People grow old by deserting their ideals.
Some one has said: "Years wrinkle the skin but to give up enthusiasm wrinkles the soul."
Youth becomes a state of mind not measured by years, but by the quality of imagination.

For two-score years, Doc did his music teaching in a small building which he called "The Noise Factory." He dreamed of the day when a new NDAC library would be erected — and the *old* library could then become the *new* music hall.

This dream became reality after Doc was gone. On May 17, 1951, the old library building was rededicated and named "Putnam Hall" in tribute to the cherished bandmaster.

41 Collector of Butterflies

FOR centuries, the cemetery had lain in tranquility beside the village of Eberbach, Germany. To the villagers it had always been the place of the dead, a place entered only by those who came to mourn. But for young Emil Krauth this graveyard held a special fascination.

Again and again, he would come there — drawn by the beautiful butterflies carved on the stone entrance. Always he pondered why it was that butterflies should be used to decorate a cemetery gate.

Finally, he learned from his pastor that the butterfly had long been a church symbol of the Resurrection — that as the caterpillar spins a cocoon about itself and stays in its dark case until the sun of springtime calls it forth in transformed beauty, so man will be called forth by the Son of God to rise from his grave in a new and glorious body.

As a youth, Emil Krauth left the village of Eberbach to study at the Art School at Karlsruhe. But ill health dogged him, and for years he sought relief at the University Clinic of Heidelberg. Physicians there shook their heads, and told him his one chance to survive was to go to a land of arid climate.

With this in mind, Krauth secured passage to America. He arrived in New York City in 1907, and was welcomed by sisters and brothers living there. Scarcely had he come there when a new malady afflicted him, and as a result, he found it difficult to sleep. He became increasingly nervous, was even fearful of losing his sanity.

To the dismay of his brothers and sisters, Emil was advised by doctors to live in the open country — preferably in the Midwest. North Dakota was suggested. His family protested that no man of education and culture could be happy in North Dakota, "a land of ice and snow, bare and void, neglected by nature, and fit only for coyotes and cowboys."

But Emil Krauth elected the prairie state, and reached Hebron one bright October day in 1907. He found the endless expanse of prairie, the incomparable sunsets to his liking.

He first tried farming, but failed because of his inexperience and his poor physical condition. The open air and sunshine, however, had a beneficial effect on his health though he continued to be scourged by sleeplessness. His greatest fear still was that he would lose his mind.

Quitting the farm, he opened a real estate and insurance office at Hebron, and continued in this business until his death at the age of 69.

One June evening as Krauth sat on the porch of his home, wondering what diversion he might find to improve his mental health, he noticed a large "silk-spinner" moth circling the porch light. Watching the moth flutter about the bulb, Emil Krauth recalled the stone-carved butterflies at Eberbach, and his boyhood fascination for butterflies was re-awakened. Perhaps even on these "barren prairies" there would be butterflies enough to provide him with a diversion that would give him a new lease on life!

His interest aroused, he sent for a book on butterflies, made a net, began to ramble about the hills surrounding Hebron to catch moths and butterflies. After each such excursion, he hurried home to his butterfly text to identify his trophies. And soon happily mounting butterflies, eager for the sunshine-and-air absorbing hours out on the prairies, Krauth felt a resurgence of life.

Noticing his zeal for finding new specimens, a few neighbors expressed the opinion that there would soon be no more different butterflies or moths for Krauth to discover. They were certain there could not be more than thirty or forty species on the North Dakota prairie.

On one of his butterfly hunts, darkness fell before Krauth returned home, and it was then that he learned there were

Leo D. Harris photo

Emil Krauth

more moths and butterflies a-wing at night than in daylight hours. So a new world was opened to him, and he spent many of the sleepless hours of night bagging the night fliers. Each summer his collection grew as he kept adding new and different specimens found living in the Hebron neighborhood.

Krauth bought more books on butterflies, subscribed to entomology magazines, and through correspondence became acquainted with other butterfly collectors. Soon he was trading his North Dakota specimens for moths and butterflies native to Asia, Africa, South America, and Europe.

It was not until Professor A. G. Arvold of the North Dakota Agricultural College happened to learn of the modest Hebron man's avocation that the public had opportunity to view the unusual collection. It was exhibited for the first time at the Fargo college.

Emil Krauth's butterfly hunts eventually took him beyond the Hebron area, and over many parts of the Northwest. He was the first to locate the Parnassus butterfly east of the Rocky Mountains. This Alpine variety, he found in the Black Hills, and on a later visit to this region, he discovered a new sub species of butterfly which has since been named in his honor: *Colias Christina Krauthii*. Today the original specimen is in the American Museum of Natural History.

In addition to collecting butterflies and moths, he also raised them, and so learned much about their habits. His library of entomology books reached a value of $2000, and his mounted butterflies and moths totaled over 10,000 specimens — a thousand of these being native to the Northwest.

As he searched the prairies for butterflies, Krauth also found Indian curios and rock specimens; these he brought home, and built up one of the largest private museums in the state. His hours of sleep were ever at a maximum of four, so on winter nights when work with his beloved butterflies was impossible, he busied himself with palette and camera, for he was an accomplished artist as well as a photographer of ability.

Emil Krauth lived his life as he once expressed it "busy

chasing butterflies instead of dollars," and so found a wealth of enjoyment of the world about him. When he died at Hebron on November 17, 1941, he left the largest private collection of moths and butterflies in America. Part of this collection may be seen at the State Historical Society museum at Bismarck; Peter S. Jungers, a Hebron attorney, owns the major part of it.

42 Schoolwoman of the Red Maxwell

THE long-awaited morning of Play Day dawned with dark clouds ominous in the sky. Charlotte, a small girl in rural Barnes County cried resolutely to her mother, "I'm going to pray to God that it won't rain today; I'm going to just *holler* to God that it won't rain!"

The skies cleared. Play Day was not spoiled for Charlotte and the many other boys and girls of the county. Buggies and wagons, that morning in June, 1908, raised clouds of dust along the dirt roads leading into Valley City. From one distant rural school came sixteen children riding in a wagon driven by their young schoolmaster. On reaching the hill overlooking the county seat, these youngsters exclaimed, "Oh, is this *Town*? Is this *Town*?" They were seeing a town for the first time. And they were enraptured when "The Whistles" — as they called the Valley City band — played.

That first Play Day in North Dakota became an annual event as gala for the children as the Fourth of July. There was always a variety of athletic contests, a parade and a pageant. One year the parade at Valley City was fifteen blocks in length. Floats of every kind represented the different schools. A rural consolidated school once appeared with each pupil riding horseback, and on a Play Day during World War I, the children of the Noltimier School paraded with half a dozen wagons loaded with scrap iron.

Play Day was but one of the innovations of Miss Minnie Jean Nielson during the term of her service — 1907 to 1919 — as superintendent of Barnes County schools. She reorganized the old-time school districts surrounding each one-room school into township-sized districts. She eliminated 44 one-room schools and created seven four-year open-country high schools.

No horse and buggy could do adequate service for the energetic Miss Nielson on her official travels from school to school. She purchased one of the first cars in Valley City. It was a bright red Maxwell. It had no top, and no windshield. "You just sat up there and drove in the wind." The car boasted acetelyne gas lamps which "You got out and lit when it began to get dark."

At times when Minnie Jean arrived at a school before nine o'clock, she would treat the pupils to a gay ride in the red Maxwell. At recess and the noon hour she would frequently repeat the treat. When it chanced that some child would say, "Grandma has never ridden in a car, and I know *she'd* like to have a ride!", the county superintendent, her day's duties done, would drive off to some farm to give Grandma her first ride in a horseless carriage.

When the phonograph was a startling new invention, Miss Nielson sponsored an entertainment in Valley City which netted funds sufficient for the purchase of an Edison Talking Machine. This marvel with its large cornucopia horn and a collection of cylinder records, she would transport from school to school. It would remain at each school for a week at a time. Once, when it was left in the care of a school board president, he and his wife sat up until midnight regaling themselves with the talking machine's delights, and their hired man sat up the rest of the night as well.

Children, grandmothers and the Edison Talking Machine were not all that this great-hearted schoolwoman carried in her red Maxwell. There was, for one thing, the traveling art

The red Maxwell is admired by pupils at a Ramsey County rural school

Dr. Minnie Jean Nielson

County Superintendent Minnie J. Nielson at the wheel of a decorated car driven in an early Play Day parade

Unloading the Noltimier School wagons filled with scrap iron following a World War I Play Day parade

exhibit. This "gallery" of twenty-four copies of old masterpieces was delivered at each school and left there for a week or two. As a result of these showings, interest was aroused and basket socials were held to obtain funds for buying good pictures to place in schoolrooms. "*Sir Galahad* was soon all over the county."

Miss Nielson learned that corn contests for school children were held up in Traill County. Corn contests were all right, she decided, but she would like something different for her county. Why not potato contests? She enlisted the aid of an NDAC horticulturist, and obtained ten seed potatoes for each interested pupil. In the fall, then, a fair was held in each township, and children entered their best specimens to be judged for prizes. Minnie Jean Nielson recalls two young boys who lugged two large sacks of giant-size "a hunk here and a bump there" potatoes to the fair at Valley City; the boys took home no prize for they found that uniformity was one of the requirements of a good potato.

The school fairs had competition in handiwork — raffia weaving, salt maps, posters, and the like. And chickens.

The latter was the outcome of another of the county superintendent's original ideas. Here, too, the trusty red Maxwell helped out.

With "a bee in her bonnet," Minnie Jean went to see the manager of the Johnson Farms Company, in southern Barnes County. Although this particular farm regularly sold Leghorn setting eggs for a dollar a dozen, the manager agreed to supply the county superintendent of schools with eggs at twenty cents a dozen for the two hundred boys and girls who wanted to take part in the project.

On a Saturday then, Miss Nielson drove her topless car out to the Johnson Company farm and loaded into it ninety crates of eggs — the initial distribution in the county. And that fall, boys and girls all over Barnes County had a cackling and crowing good time exhibiting their Leghorn hens and roosters at township fairs.

In late autumn, Miss Nielson would escort, by train, to

an institute at NDAC, the pupils who had placed first in the final county competitions. She recalls with pleasure an incident en route with a group of eleven boys and girls. When the young backcountry folk were all settled on the upholstered, red-velvet seats of the coach, Maggie Dettmer — voicing the impressions of all — joyously exclaimed, "Oh, Heaven must be like this!" Then, on arrival at the Gardner Hotel in Fargo — where Miss Nielson had been able to obtain special-rate rooms — they truly believed they had entered Paradise itself.

When Minnie Jean Nielson's name appeared on her party's ticket as a candidate for the office of state superintendent of public instruction, the opposition labeled her a "pink tea society lady." But, regardless, this efficient woman was the only member of her party to be elected to office that fall.

One of her innovations as state superintendent was the practice of holding county superintendent institutes in some historic place in the state rather than in one of the larger cities. Always intensely loyal to North Dakota, she never missed an opportunity to develop that sentiment in other citizens.

It was during her eight-year administration that North Dakota was made a PTA Demonstration State by the National PTA Office. Miss Nielson appointed Mrs. Emma Golden of Zeeland to travel over the state, working with county superintendents to organize local PTAs — and membership rose to 30,000 in the state. National PTA officials were so gratified that they later drafted Miss Nielson to do field work in several states.

As state superintendent, Miss Nielson adopted as her slogan, "No illiteracy in North Dakota" and, to that end, she saw that night schools were organized in every county, to teach illiterates to read and write. The only man in Nelson County unable to sign his name knew no peace so long as he remained there. He was a hired man and fled from farm to farm, ever pursued by some teacher — infected by Miss Nielson's zeal — bent on making him literate, and Nelson County 100 per cent so.

Due to the illness of her mother, Minnie Jean retired from the state office to remain at home. When her sister at length returned from work in France, Miss Nielson was free to accept a position as field representative of the National Illiteracy Crusade headed by Cora Wilson Stewart. She spoke at universities and colleges in 42 states, exhorting teachers to eradicate illiteracy.

During a two-month investigation in Kentucky, she found there were 10,000 illiterates in one county alone. She visited schools where there was not one library book, not one picture on the schoolroom wall. She returned to North Dakota feeling that education in her home state was "right out front."

After two strenuous years with the National Illiteracy Crusade, Miss Nielson came home to Valley City and served twelve years as secretary of the North Dakota Teachers Insurance and Retirement Fund. On resigning in 1950, she had rounded out 45 years of educational service — a career begun when yet under sixteen, she had pinned up her pigtails to become a teacher in District 9 of Barnes County.

Many well-deserved honors have been bestowed upon this schoolwoman. Fargo College, in 1919, conferred a Doctor of Laws degree upon her in recognition of her achievements as an educator and for her work as state director of Liberty Loan drives during World War I. She was the first woman elected as delegate to a national presidential nominating convention, and the first woman from North Dakota to be listed in "Who's Who."

She organized the first statewide convention of social work in North Dakota. She has held many leading offices in educational, fraternal and club organizations.

Miss Nielson embarked on a new venture, in 1953, when she became president of the Sheyenne Royalty Company — an all-woman oil corporation investing in mineral acres. This first women's oil company in the state now includes "a few husbands and even some bachelors."

This "go-getting" lady frankly admits she is past the retirement age, but not yet ready to retire. At Valley City, she lives in the old family home — a brown, gabled house on Central Avenue — with her sister Hazel, also a notable educator, and her sister-in-law, Mrs. Esther Clark Nielson, a home economics teacher.

43 "Prairie Pictures" Creator

MORE than half a million "Prairie Pictures" deck homes in America and in other lands. In North Dakota one hangs on a wall in almost every home — for it is here that the unique creation originated, here that the native daughter creator still produces them.

Ida Bisek, as a toddler, rejoiced in the form and color of the poppies, the zinnias and the marigolds in her mother's little garden; and, as she grew, a longing to transplant their beauty onto canvas became a passion.

But there was never a surplus in the family funds to provide her with needed paints and brushes. And so, because she had no paints, Ida Bisek did what no one yet had done — she created pictures from feathers.

The feathers she first used were from the game birds that her father and brothers brought in for the Bisek table. The girl saw in the feathers too much beauty to destroy, and so she salvaged the most colorful of them, and experimented with arranging feather tips to form flower designs. Soon she was assembling bouquets of them laid flat upon pieces of cardboard and covered with glass. Framed, the unique pictures became Ida's gifts to her friends.

When she was fifteen, she began work at the Lidgerwood post office; her $10-a-month salary provided her with the long-coveted brushes, oils and canvas. By the time she was 23, she was a classified civil service employee, her wages contributed to the family support; her spare time always found her busy with her art mediums.

At 29 she was married to Charles Prokop, and became mistress of a spacious Lidgerwood home. The large yard stimulated her interest in flowers, and awakened a desire to sculpture figures for a formal garden setting. By the trial and error method she produced creditable life-size statues of herons, swans and human forms.

In 1939 North Dakota was celebrating its Golden Anniversary and Ida wanted to sculpture something special — something historically commemorative — for the Lidgerwood Federated clubs when they would entertain 25 neighboring clubs.

Thus the "Daughters of Dakota" came into being. The first of Ida Prokop's notable sculptures, this bas-relief was created in the basement laundry room of her home. Mrs. Ruth Seekins and her small daughter Patricia were the models for the work.

Using raw clay dug near her home, Mrs. Prokop made the original model in deep relief, half life size. Plaster was poured over this clay model to form a mould. Then when the mould had hardened, the clay was removed, and casting plaster poured into the mould. Once the casting plaster had set, the mould was chipped from the bas-relief. Coated with gold-bronze paint, it was ready for unveiling at the Lidgerwood club convention.

"Daughters of Dakota" aroused much interest among the assembled club women. Because of their interest, this original bas-relief was placed in the Liberty Memorial Building at Bismarck, and Mrs. Prokop was brought in contact with North Dakotans who encouraged her to develop her talents.

After the unveiling of "Daughters of Dakota" at Bismarck, Ida Prokop drove out to a clay deposit near Mandan and procured a thousand pounds of the clay. Home at Lidgerwood, she experimented not only with clay, but with paints, water colors, a new air brush, and the little feather pictures friends welcomed as gifts and prizes.

That summer, the manager of a little souvenir store at Chahinkapa Park, Wahpeton, decided to try marketing a few of Ida's feather miniatures. They sold readily. And after a salesman, stopping at this store, asked if he might show a few of them to other North Dakota storekeepers on his route, Ida Prokop suddenly found herself in business.

Almost daily, that fall of 1941, she received store orders from merchants over both the Dakotas. Shortly the Prokop basement was transformed into a production center for "Dakota Prairie Pictures" — pictures that were new and novel to an enthusiastic public, but something Ida had experimented with for twenty years.

Her 70-year old father cut the picture frames in the furnace room. Glass was cut and polished in the laundry. Ida's easel was set up in the drying room; the bouquet compositions were assembled in the den. The hallway was stacked with packing boxes and excelsior. There was no need for a storeroom since Ida and her crew of six were unable to keep up with the orders.

Funds secured from the sale of the Prairie Pictures now enabled Ida Prokop to undertake another artistic project — the sculpturing of an authentic male and female portrait bust to represent each of five major North Dakota Indian tribes. The busts would be a gift to the North Dakota Historical Society — a legacy from one Dakota prairie daughter.

She did the first work on her Indian project at the Wahpeton Indian School. Her models were Gregory Des Jarlies, a Cree boy; Esther Frenier, a Sioux girl; and Mrs. Robert Horne, a teacher at the school, and a great-great granddaughter of Sakakawea.

But just when Ida Prokop was making happy progress with the sculpturing, and the production of her Dakota Prairie Pictures was prospering, she discovered that she was breaking a state law. This particular law prohibited "the sale or barter of any part thereof of a protected game bird, including the skin with the plumage thereon." Pheasants, which

Ida Prokop Lee
at work in her
Prairie Pictures Studio

"Chipping" the bust of
Choke Cherry Woman

"Ida Lee" lampshade (which makes use
of Prairie Pictures technique) mounted on
a base of Dakota Driftwood

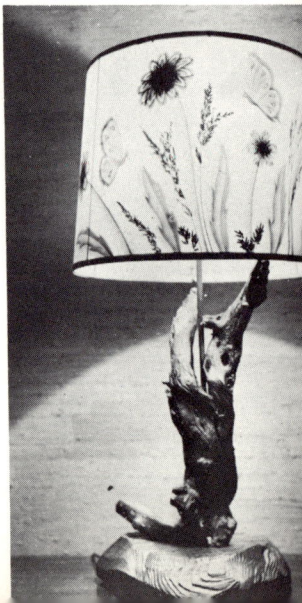

Views of Ida Prokop Lee's
Indian sculpture

provided the most desirable of all feathers for the pictures were "protected game birds" in North Dakota.

She arranged to have a Minnesota farmer raise pheasants for her, then found that the pheasant feathers were subject to North Dakota law as soon as they were brought into the State. Ida Prokop began to wonder whether she would be permitted to keep a barrel of clay with her in a jail cell.

In September, 1942, she went to Bismarck to make a bust of Governor John Moses. She told her distinguished model how the long arm of North Dakota law, specifically the State Fish and Game Department, had just a few days earlier apprehended her as an offender. The Governor was much interested and sympathetic.

The clay model of the Moses bust wrapped in damp cloth and stowed in her car, Ida went to the Capitol in response to the official summons of E. M. Lee, Chief Game Warden. His department expressed sympathy, paid tribute to her craft, but summarily informed her she could place no more Prairie Pictures on the market until the state law so permitted.

Her next "project" was to lobby a special law permitting pen propagation of upland birds. While she lobbied at Bismarck, she worked on another Indian model — Judge Frank B. Zahn (Flying Cloud). Her bill was passed by the Legislature, and signed by Governor Moses — and Ida Prokop was able to resume production of the feather pictures.

She found her next Indian models at the Fort Berthold Indian Reservation. These were Crows Heart, Mrs. Sitting Crow and Chief Drags Wolf. Only thirty days after the mask of his face had been completed, Drags Wolf was dead.

At Fort Yates, Lena Bullhead Longchase, daughter of Red Tomahawk, served as another model. The same winter, Chief Little White Cloud, a Chippewa visiting at Lidgerwood, gladly posed for her. In the summer of 1944, Mrs. Prokop returned to the Fort Berthold Reservation, and modeled two Arikaras — Hanna Fox (Cherry Woman) and a young Marine, Perry Ross (Two Sticks), who had been blinded in a South Pacific battle and was home on furlough.

On October 25, 1943 the Governor Moses bust of copper bronze was formally presented to the State Historical Society in an impressive ceremony at Liberty Memorial Building. Two years later, Moses, then a U. S. Senator, passed away.

Following a special session of the North Dakota legislature in 1944, L. L. Twitchell, long-time legislator died suddenly. His friends at the Capitol persuaded Mrs. Prokop to make a post mortem bust. This was done, and at the next session of the legislature, the bust was dedicated and mounted on a native granite boulder at the entrance to the House of Representatives.

A. M. Christensen of Minot, in honoring two of his former college professors at NDAC, commissioned her to model Dr. H. L. Bolley and Dr. L. R. Waldron. The busts were unveiled and presented to the College at its Golden Anniversary graduation ceremonies.

A third NDAC scientist, Dr. C. B. Waldron, was likewise memorialized when the State Horticultural Society obtained Mrs. Prokop's services in producing a likeness of this tree-planting apostle of outdoor beauty.

Meanwhile, the production of Prairie Pictures outgrew the basement quarters, and was moved into a commercial building. The original crew of six had increased to twenty-five.

Divorced from her first husband, Mrs. Prokop — in 1947 — married E. M. Lee, the Chief Game Warden she first had met with such trepidation. They established their home five miles north of Valley City, in the valley of the Sheyenne. Here, at their "Shy-Soo Ranch" they also built a new Prairie Pictures studio.

One of the four replicas of the original "Daughters of Dakota" is imbedded in the redwood wall above the fireplace in the Lee home. Close by is the studio building where Ida Prokop Lee continues to design new Prairie Pictures and to work on her Indian sculpture.

Success in native crafts has not caused her to rest on her laurels. In recent years, she has produced "Dakota Driftwood," begun the milling and distributing of Dakota Clay, and originated a new product — translucent lamp shades decorated with the feather-flower bouquets.

Recently, the Lees bought a Piper Cub plane and acquired private pilot's licenses. During the fall of 1953, Ida Lee enrolled in a ceramics course at the University of North Dakota — and flew to classes at Grand Forks.

As long as she lives, there is little chance that Ida Prokop Lee's "ten stubby fingers" will ever be idle.

44 North Dakota's Ace Athlete

CASPER Oimoen is a bricklaying contractor who does his work with a craftsman's thoroughness. Minot folks who obtain his services may little realize that a few decades ago this bricklayer was lauded as the nation's greatest skier, and his name often headlined the sports sections of great dailies.

In his home at Minot may be seen the 20 medals and more than 400 trophies awarded Oimoen during his athletic career.

As a small boy in Norway, he first learned to ski on barrel staves. At ten he took part in his first ski jump tournament at Raufoss. Then in 1927, a youth of seventeen, he brought a few of his ski trophies with him to America, came to Minot to live with an uncle, O. P. Nustad, and began learning the bricklayer's trade.

For two years, Casper was occupied with mortar and brick. Then in January, 1925, he went to Fargo where he entered and won his first ski competition in America. The same month he went to Canton, South Dakota, to enter the boys' event of a national ski tournament. He spilled his first time down, but on the next he jumped 183 feet — which was 27 feet farther than that cleared by the Class A champion.

Casper Oimoen, national ski champion

He went on to Minneapolis and there won the Northwest Class B championship. Next, at the St. Paul Winter Carnival ski tournament, he won first place. And for ten years thereafter, the name of Casper Oimoen was familiar to ski enthusiasts all over America.

In 1926, this Minot bricklayer entered the Northwest Championship competition at Glenwood Park, Minneapolis. Seven years he won first place there.

Deciding to visit his parents in Norway, Casper took part in several ski tourneys there during 1927. At the Midstubakken meet, he was third in competition with 350 of Norway's top skiers.

A summary of Oimoen's remarkable record is to be found in *The History of the National Ski Association and the Ski Sport* published in 1931: "Central champion from 1925 to 1931, Eastern division champion, 1930; National champion 1930 and 1931, comprising two National championships, seven Central division championships, one Eastern division championship, six hill records, six times most graceful rider, and two State championships." He later won the National Championship for 1933.

How he could capture more than 400 trophies and medals in less than fifteen years can be understood when one considers his accomplishments during the year 1931:

First place, hill record of 169 feet, Gary Indiana

First place, hill record of 174 feet, Chicago

First place, Central championship, Minneapolis

First place, National championship, Canton, South Dakota

First place, hill record of 161 feet, Greenfield, Massachusetts

First place, Eastern championship, Claremont, New Hampshire

First place, most graceful rider, Rutland, Vermont

First place, most graceful rider, Bear Mountain, New York

First place, hill record of 187 feet at Lake Placid, New York

One of the highlights of Oimoen's career took place at the Big Pines Winter Sports Carnival in California, February, 1935. Here, before 20,000 spectators, he made the longest jump of his life — 255 feet. With this, he established a new American Amateur record, and won for himself the Western American ski jumping championship.

His most daring feat was at Salt Lake City that same year. He was one of four skiers who swooped down the hill in close formation, and jumped together, each one clearing more than 200 feet. They accomplished this twice without mishap, then agreed that they would never do it again.

A week later, at Anaconda, Montana, while preparing for the introduction of night skiing, Casper jumped 185 feet and broke his right leg. Never again did North Dakota's ace athlete enter a ski competition.

45 World's Champion Miniature Writer

BACK in 1926, James W. Zaharee, a Max farm lad, bruised and bashed himself in a motorcycle accident. While hospitalized, the boy entered upon a career that was to win him world fame.

A fad sweeping America at that time was the "small-writing" contest. Jim found numbers of such contests described and advertised in the magazines his friends and relatives brought him. These contests offered prizes for writing the largest number of letters or figures within a defined small area.

Happy for something to amuse him, Jim tried his hand at a number of such small-writing contests. To his surprise, he won several; his interest in learning to write smaller was whetted, and he entered more of the contests.

Thus it happened that during the drouth years, when most farmers in western North Dakota raised little besides dust and Russian Thistle, this farm youth — by writing very, very small — won numerous prizes, including five different automobiles.

Jim Zaharee decided to make miniature writing his career. For a short time he attended Minot State Teachers College, then for three years studied engineering and design at the University of Michigan.

In 1935, Bob Ripley declared Zaharee to be the world's champion miniature writer after Jim had written 9007 letters on a single grain of rice. A few years later he bettered this record when he wrote the entire Declaration of Independence — plus the names of its 56 signers and the names of the thirteen original colonies — all on one side of a grain of rice. This was a total of 7576 legible letters of such minute size that they could be read only with the aid of a microscope. The writing was not done in a day — Zaharee worked at this unique project for eight months.

He can write a 20,000-letter composition in the space of a postage stamp. He once wrote 101 verses of the "Rubaiyat" by Omar Khayyam in a book that was one-eighth of an inch square, and 1/32 of an inch thick. It took him four months to complete this 26-page book.

At the Dallas, Texas, Centennial Exposition in 1936, Zaharee did some miniature writing on human hair. He wrote Lincoln's Gettysburg Address on a single strand of hair no longer than 2¼ inches.

There is nothing magical about Zaharee's accomplishment. He taught himself. His skill was acquired by patient practice in training his muscles, nerves and eyes. As a result of his training and practice, he is able to read a newspaper eight feet away.

For his finest writing, he uses crow-quill pen points which he sharpens to points eight to 24 times finer than a hair. He

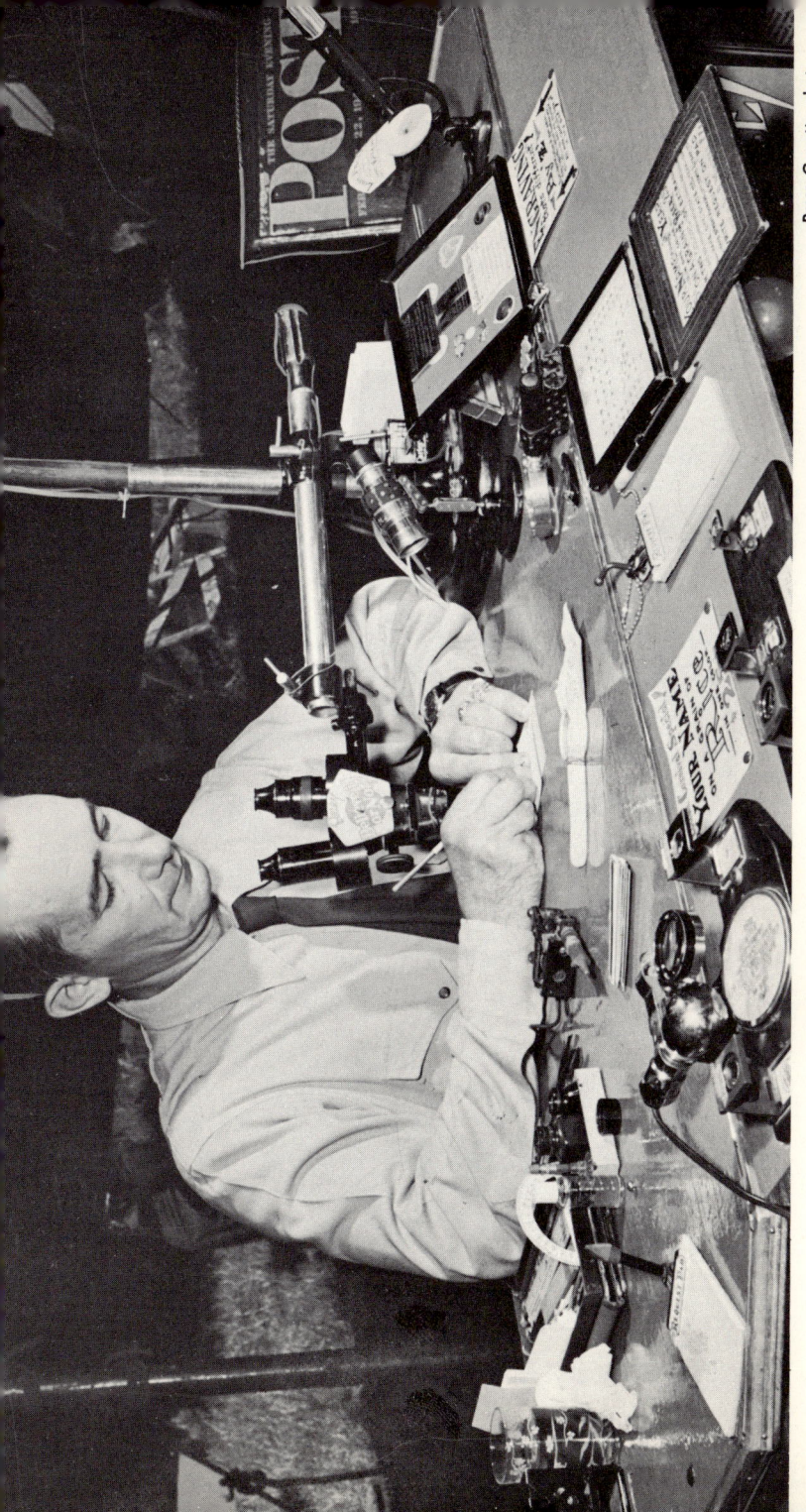

James W. Zaharee doing his "Believe It Or Not" writing on a grain of rice

Press Gazette photo

uses ordinary ink. To enable him to see what he is doing, he makes use of a binocular-type electrically-lighted microscope. He requires absolute quiet in the house where he is working — should someone walk across the floor, the steps would cause vibrations sufficient to damage his writing. He cannot work near the seashore for even the reverberations of waves affect the infinitely fine lines of his penmanship. Some of his best work has been done out on the quiet prairie farm near Max, late at night.

At expositions and fairs, he writes the names of individuals on grains of rice. This is a simple task for Zaharee. He first glues a grain of polished rice into a depression in a small card. He inscribes the name without the aid of magnifying lens, then lacquers the rice so it will not deteriorate. Thousands of people all over America have these souvenir proofs of Zaharee's skill; he has written millions of characters on rice.

Among famous persons who have had Zaharee write their names on a grain of rice are Jack Dempsey, Jean Hersholt, Bing Crosby and the late President Franklin Roosevelt. For Zaharee, one of the most memorable inscriptions was for Amelia Earhart just a few days before she flew to her death in the Pacific.

Jim's first public demonstration was when Bob Ripley featured him in the "Ripley Odditorium" opening on Broadway, and later playing at three expositions. Except for 42 months with the Navy and 24 with the Marines during World War II, Zaharee has been exhibiting his phenomenal skill ever since Ripley first brought him to public attention.

Several times he has acted as Cupid, and written proposals on rice for timid suitors. He has frequently inscribed love songs on rice, the Lord's Prayer on rice or some small treasured article. Occasionally, in prankish mood, he may write to a friend on a grain of rice or a length of hair. Reading the "letter" is the recipient's problem.

46 "Telle," Woodcarver

JUST off Highway 10, in the village of McKenzie, is a little cream-colored house with the sign "Woodcarvings" upon its roof, and a circular sign on the front wall announcing that here is "Telle's Hobby Lab." On the double doors of the small garage nearby is a generous sample of Telle's ability to paint Norwegian "Rosemalling."

The "Telle" used by Miss Thelma Rudser as her trade name was given as a nickname by her family. She was also dubbed "Squaw Whittle Sticks" by her brothers during those practice years at the work which has earned for her a distinctive place in the field of creative art. But under any name, this woman possesses the true artist's love for her special, God-given medium of expression, and is unwaveringly dedicated to authenticity in her "Norsk-Kraft" wood carving.

It was two large ladles carved by her grandfather which first inspired Telle to make a specialty of Norwegian-design woodcarving. Artistry in wood was truly an inheritance. Her great uncle Sevil had been a cabinet maker in Norway. Another great uncle, Thomas Risem, did carving for the Chickering Piano Company, and was at one time commissioned by a Boston millionaire to carve a table for the W. K. Vanderbilt family.

Make your way to Telle's little house and you will find her — in jeans and a plaid shirt — at her workbench busy with knife or chisel. There is no lack of orders for her work; folks keep dropping in with some special request. She has carved salad fork-and-spoon sets with patterns to match the owners' Sterling silverware. She carves missing parts for treasured antique furniture.

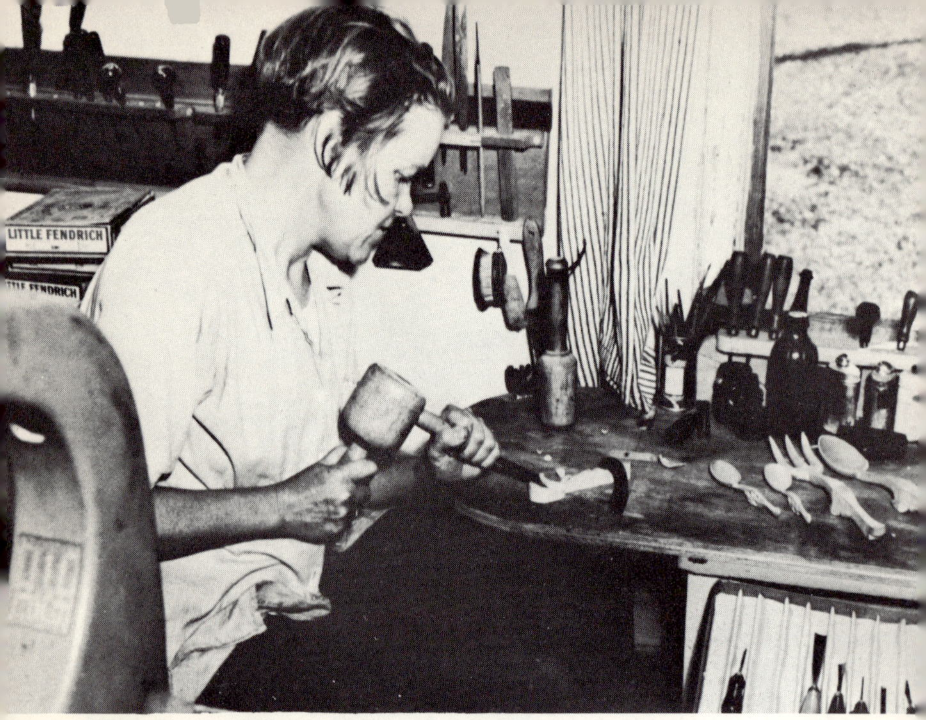

"Telle" at her workbench.
Conrad Publishing Company photo

"Norsk-Kraft" carvings
by Telle

Telle's Hobby Lab
at McKenzie

"Martha by the Day"
　　　Risem Studio photo

"Greasemonkey Pete"
　　　Risem Studio photo

"Waiting for the Galloping Goose"
　　　Risem Studio photo

Once a lady brought her an old sepia print showing a three-year-old boy holding his pet dog; the dog's head was somewhat blurred — but Telle was asked to carve that little dog for a Father's Day gift for the boy — now 67 years old. When the daughter presented Telle's carving to him, he immediately recognized his childhood pet.

Born at Grand Forks, Thelma Rudser began whittling when she was six years old. That same year her next-door neighbors packed to move away and found among their discards two jack knives which they gave to Thelma. Her older brother promptly traded her out of the better knife — but with the other, dull as it was, she whittled away with great satisfaction.

When she was fourteen, Telle attempted her first piece of serious woodcarving, a case for a dresser clock. Always a dog lover, she began carving dogs in the round. Her first public exhibit — at a hobby show — was a set of 24 miniature dogs in a little glass-covered kennel.

Tiny lapel dogs which she carved provided her with spending money when she was a University coed. During her Junior year, she bought her first set of woodcarving chisels and produced her earliest figurines.

Following graduation from the University in 1934, Miss Rudser taught school, served as a recreation leader in the Grand Forks park system, and did considerable work as a crafts specialist.

In this latter work, she traveled over North Dakota and occasionally happened upon individuals she thought would make good subjects for figurines of wood.

It was while breakfasting at a Killdeer cafe that she espied "Grease Monkey Pete." Quickly, she got a piece of paper from her purse, began sketching the man. A cafe customer sitting beside her perceived what she was doing, and cooperated by detaining Grease Monkey Pete long enough for Telle to get his likeness on paper.

At another time, she was waiting for a train at Beulah when a picturesque old couple settled down opposite her.

They sat there together without exchanging a word. Thelma took out a piece of paper, and had only the man sketched by the time her train arrived. Fortunately, the pair got on the train with her. Halfway between Sanger and Hensler, the train came to a halt, was reported out of fuel. So, for the next forty minutes while the train stood still, Telle completed the sketch which was to result in "Waiting for the Galloping Goose."

Another piece of amusing portraiture in wood was "Martha by the Day." The subject worked for Miss Rudser's landlady, receiving 25 cents an hour for doing laundry and cleaning. A work-worn individual, she was flabbergasted when Telle paid her a dollar for posing — just standing still at the ironing board!

A patriot as well as an artist, Thelma joined the Waves in November of 1943. During her boot training at Hunter College, her entire collection of woodcarvings — including the three pieces mentioned — was stolen.

For two years, she worked as an aviation machinist's mate, and pondered her woodcarving. Discharged in 1945, she decided she could not give up the craft that had brought her some of the greatest satisfactions in her life. She lived in a rented bedroom at Bismarck for a while, did her carving in a corner of the room.

To make her living from woodcarving, Miss Rudser realized that she would have to find a home where living costs could be kept at the minimum. Accordingly, in 1948, she purchased a run-down little house at McKenzie, and largely through her own labors, has converted it into her present "Hobby Lab."

And there in the little house beside the highway, Telle sits at her work bench. She lives frugally, but hers is the great satisfaction of doing the work she likes best to do. The handsomely-carved plates of all sizes, the nut bowls, salad sets, the exquisite letter knives with tiny elves surmounting hilts, the sword-like *lefse* turners, the unique brooches, tie-chains and ear rings — all attest that Telle has long since surpassed the skill of the ancestors who first inspired her.

47 Crochet Specialist

EUGENE Nelson's crocheted bedspreads and Cluny lace tablecloths have taken blue ribbons at the Grand Forks State Fair. Two of his bedspreads have won Honorable Mention in national crocheting contests — one such competition having over 400,000 entries.

This dairy farmer's specialty had its beginning 56 years ago — when he was twelve, and Bertina Everson, the hired girl, was teaching his two sisters to crochet. Fascinated by the craft, Eugene borrowed a crocheting needle, and Bertina added him to her class.

Eugene grew to manhood on the Manvel farm, milking cows, tilling the soil, and crocheting. For a time, he and his brother Nels were bachelors together on the home farm. Eugene decided that if he had to cook, he might as well learn more than just frying pan rudiments. Eventually, he was taking from the oven pastries as fine-textured and delectable as any housewife could turn out—all with no neglect of his crocheting.

By 1927 — the year he took unto himself a bride — his Lady Baltimore cake with whipped cream topping was something the local Ladies Aid discussed with envying admiration. Whenever the new Mrs. Eugene Nelson carried to one of their food bazaars any of her husband's superior baking, the women had a fast-selling special.

The master crocheter, however, was doing more — much more — than dividing his time between baking and lace making. There were his fifteen cows to milk, his 240 acres to tend. The needlework of his leisure hours included other than that done with a crocheting needle. For the versatile and industrious farmer learned tailoring and dressmaking. Several brides of the vicinity have worn, with great pride,

The crochet specialist relaxing in his favorite rocker

Eugene Nelson and some of his handiwork

wedding dresses stitched by Eugene Nelson. In gratitude for those early crocheting lessons, he has sewn dresses for each of the six daughters of Bertina — Mrs. George Udenby.

Evenings on the Manvel farm, especially during the winter, are usually given to crochet work. As Eugene Nelson sat in his favorite rocker — in earlier years — and transformed balls of thread into patterned webs, there was the happy sound of an infant son's cooing, the static and music from the new-fangled radio.

The son has now assumed major responsibility of managing the farm and the senior Nelson has more time for the pursuit of his hobbies — hobbies that fill the hours gainfully as well as pleasantly. He and his wife engage in the craft of rug-weaving; as many as a hundred yards of rag rugs come annually from the Nelson loom. The rugs, in quality, are on par with Eugene's lace and pastry.

Another joint accomplishment has been the baking of *lefse*. During Thanksgiving and Christmas seasons, Mr. and Mrs. Nelson bake, for sale, between forty and fifty dozen of the tasty potato cakes.

The evenings on the Nelson farm have changed but little through the years. The son has grown up, and the radio has become commonplace, but the crocheting specialist still rocks in his favorite chair and works at a doily or more ambitious piece of lace. The season may be winter and harsh winds may be abroad, but indoors is the contentment and calm that are the portion of those who lose themselves in creative pursuit.

48 A Few Other Hobbyists

THE Eugene Nelsons have a couple of neighbors who have interesting hobbies. Archie Brown is, by avocation, a Nimrod — "a mighty hunter"; and he has an extraordinary collection of guns and cartridges, and mounted trophies of the hunt. Louis J. Braaten paints in oils and does taxidermy; and he has, for almost two decades, made violins.

Some of the state's collectors have passed the hobby stage and reached museum status. Outstanding among these is Henry Klebe, at Lake Metigoshee State Park, north of Bottineau. His collection has many pioneer curios, Indian artifacts, and fossils.

Frank G. Johnson of Fullerton has his hobby-trove on display in a specially-constructed building in the backyard of his home. In that interesting assortment of historical objects are such as: a collection of over 2000 different kinds of buttons; over 2000 arrowheads; 150 stone Indian hammers; 106 old guns — including three flintlocks of Revolutionary days.

H. J. Rustad's rare accumulation of a sixty-year period of collecting started when he — at ten — was fascinated by a Norwegian coin that he found. All his historical treasure is housed in a two-room building at Kindred. There are assorted Norwegian antiques. There are Indian weapons and cooking utensils. One sees there mounted birds, church bells, harness-making tools, fossils and "other items too numerous to mention."

And he who would go sleuthing over the state will be surprised at the number of interesting collections — and hobby-ists — he will find!

Archie A. Brown with his collection of guns and mounted trophies of the hunt

Frank G. Johnson in his private museum at Fullerton

49 The Clever-Handed Kotschevars

WHEN the depression came, Mr. and Mrs. H. J. Kotschevar took-to-the-hills. Up in the Turtle Mountains, near Dunseith, they built a dream home that has turned into a show place.

Native logs served them for their four-room house, and seasoned poplar for the furniture. With a pocket knife as his principal tool, Mr. Kotschevar shaped and decorated the pieces — which include, besides chairs, a davenport, tables and a radio cabinet. Some idea of the patient skill that went into the making of these pieces is gained from the fact that one particular chair required 300 hours of whittling time.

Along with the functional pieces of their "Deer Heart Lodge" are some unique show pieces. A miniature log house — about 3½ feet long — is roofed with hand-whittled shingles that total 3000; it is completely furnished in nicely scaled models, and inhabited by a family of mounted mice. (Taxidermy is one of Mrs. Kotschevar's hobbies.) Another type of oddity among the many that attract tourists and elicit their exclamations, is the three-dimension scenes in which mounted frogs represent people. One of these depicts WPA workers — leaning on their shovels; another, Major Bowes' orchestra; and a third, a table of poker players.

The landscaped grounds of Deer Heart Lodge bear further testimony of what loving care and knowing hands can accomplish. Here are walls made of stones mortared together, a rustic bridge over a little stream, and — wholly decorative, a miniature chateau built of variously-colored stones from the locality. The profusion of flowers and the fruitfulness of certain trees considered by most North Dakotans as not adaptable to the region convince all viewers that on the couple's clever hands are green thumbs.

Mr. and Mrs. H. J. Kotschevar seated in their Deer Heart Lodge, Dunseith

The miniature chateau at Deer Heart Lodge

View showing grounds at Deer Heart Lodge.
Note unique stone-and-mortar bridge.

50 Artist in a Henhouse

"HALF the chickencoop is yours — if you can make it do," Harry Olson told his son-in-law.

Young Joe Messer considered the henhouse. He saw that at least it could provide roof and walls for a place where he — a trained potter — might launch upon a career in ceramics.

He knew that his earnings at the Farmers Union Elevator at Bowman could never supply sufficient funds to purchase quarters and the necessary equipment for a pottery-making project. But this smelly old chickencoop could well make first substance of his dreams.

So the hens were displaced to the second section of the long, low building. Then Joe and his wife Eunice removed the roosts, the nests and the feed troughs from the hens' first home and scrubbed the place clean.

They sold their cow and their furniture, and were glad they could share the Harry Olson home. They would need every penny they could scrape together before they could produce "Ceramics by Messer." Joe realized they lacked money for buying regulation equipment, but he figured that where there's a will, there's a way.

He set to work on the first of the two required kilns. Lacking experience, he had to construct the kiln chimney three times before it would draw properly. He built and rebuilt and adjusted the kiln burners dozens of times before they functioned to his satisfaction. Weeks passed in the construction of these two kilns — for all the brick used had to be shaped by hand.

After rummaging in auto junk piles, Joe came home with an old Ford transmission. This he set upright on a stand and

Messer pottery of native clays

Sculptured bust of his wife by Joseph Messer

Messer ceramics in western Dakota designs

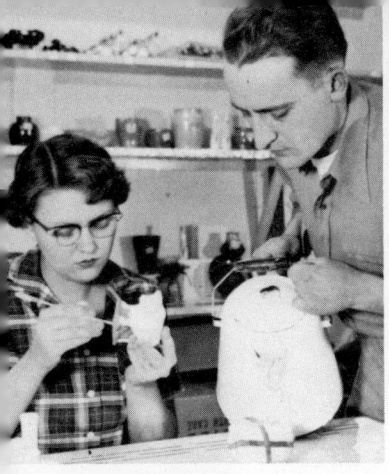

Husband-and-wife team at work. Eunice brushes on glaze, Joe pours "slip" into mold.

Joseph Messer

Joseph Messer "throwing" a vase

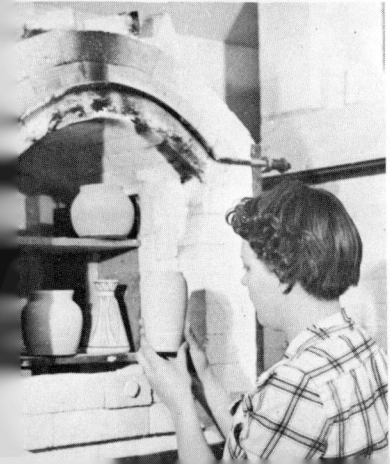

Eunice Messer placing pottery in kiln for firing

powered with an electric motor. The result was a Messer-designed potter's wheel that Joe could operate at three speeds forward and one in reverse — and he decided that it was quite an improvement over the classic, centuries-old, foot-powered potter's wheel.

He took discarded files and screw drivers, and fashioned tools for use in making hand-thrown vases and designing original clay models. Resourcefulness and ingenuity had to compensate for lack of funds many times before this unique little plant in the western North Dakota ranchlands was ready for production in the fall of 1952.

Born in Buffalo Springs, Joe had come to the Bowman community when he was just a toddler. After graduating from the Bowman high school, he served three years in the U. S. Navy. On receiving his discharge from service, he returned to Bowman and married Eunice Olson. He went then for study at the Kansas City Art Institute at Kansas City, Missouri, and was graduated with honors in 1951. He majored in oil painting, and also studied sculpturing and ceramics. Home again, he worked at the elevator until he acquired the makeshift studio.

Joe, that autumn of 1952, began designing and producing pieces that were typical of his region — models of Hereford and Black Angus cattle, antelope and prairie dogs. Because he preferred a porcelain finish for his pottery, he used clays imported from Pennsylvania — clays that could be fired to 2500 degrees Fahrenheit. The beautifully-glazed Messer ceramics caught the eye of the westerner — and Joe dared believe he could make his livelihood from the art which claimed his heart.

For a while, though, he and Eunice could not even afford a door to their studio. One day, during that time, a hen decided to return to her former domicile. When Joe discovered the intruder, she was standing in the middle of the studio floor, appraising the shelves of fragile porcelain with obvious intent of selecting a spot to roost.

Gently, very gently, Joe tried to shoo the Plymouth Rock out the way she came in. But she was a single-minded bird, and the more Joe shooed, the more insistent she was on reaching the desired spot. Suddenly she took flight and made a wing-flapping landing amidst the pottery.

Porcelain fragments splattered from the shelf. Ever since Joe has had increased relish for broiled chicken.

One night a skunk got into the chicken pen attached to the east side of the studio. Aroused by the commotion that followed, Joe and Eunice ran out and with a flashlight spotted the marauder. Joe took careful aim with the shotgun and ended the skunk's life — but not its odor. For several weeks thereafter, studio visitors sniffed the air questioningly, and Joe and Eunice worked resolutely, in the laden atmosphere, to fill increasing orders for "Ceramics by Messer."

After experimenting with different North Dakota clays, Joe found that many of the native clays would produce interesting and sometimes very attractive natural glazes if applied to the surface of a piece and fired at higher temperatures than usually was needed.

He designed a series of North Dakota wild life pieces to add to his ash trays, salt and pepper shakers, and other commercial items.

The first autumn Joe and Eunice Messer had their plant in full-time operation, a salesman placed their wares in a number of stores and so many orders resulted that Joe had little time left for his pastime of hunting and trapping. By early summer of 1953, they needed more working space. So the hens had to move again to give the Messer studio another room of equal size.

Gradually, with one improvement after another, the henhouse has lost all the marks of its original use. The hens have now been evacuated from the building.

Joe hasn't designed any porcelain biddies, but ranchers and farmers over the Northwest proudly display in their homes art objects that give them special joy. These are Joe's gleaming porcelain models of livestock and of wild life, the gracefully-wrought vases and planters of native clay. As Joe explains, "My aim is to make the owner feel that here is his native soil brought into his house and made beautiful and useful by the skill of human hands."

51 Rural School Godmother

A DEAFENING crash, a split-second flash of burning light, and the little Traill County rural school had been struck by lightning. The stove pipe hurtled to the floor, fell apart. Soot exploded into the air, cascaded over teacher, pupils and all else.

Youngest among the terrified children were the twins, Lloyd and Leila Ewen, seated in the second row. Half-stunned, they groped their way out of the schoolhouse while the teacher, Miss Christine Koppang, urged her flock forth, fearful that the building might catch fire.

In the pouring rain, the children beheld each others' soot-blackened faces and burst into laughter. Then they fled to the nearest farm home, a quarter of a mile away.

Here, Mrs. Dave McCulloch welcomed the grimy, drenched youngsters with sympathy and understanding. She brought a large tin tub into the kitchen, filled it with water for the girls; and prepared another one in another room for the boys. Shortly the pupils of Blanchard School were scrubbed clean, and outfitted with dry clothing from the closets of the McCulloch home.

For Leila C. Ewen, the experience was the first of many memorable ones in the environs of a little white prairie schoolhouse. Now considered one of North Dakota's leading educators, she has made a career out of bettering the education of children from farm homes.

During Leila's childhood, her father was manager of the Smith Farm, one of the large wheat farms in the Red River Valley. When he resigned this position, he purchased a farm two miles south of Mayville; but shortly after the home was completed and the farm developed, he passed away.

From then on Mrs. Ewen and her four children shared the responsibilities of the farm. Industrious Leila helped indoors and out — did housework, milked cows, carried food to men working in the fields, did most of the saddle work, and ran errands.

She could handle any horse on the place. Although timid girl friends may have quaked inwardly as they rode in the buggy with her behind some spirited horse, they yet were confident that Leila would keep the animal under control. Once, on the way home from town, Leila's horse was frightened, reared, tangled himself in the harness and fell down. Leila jumped from the buggy and calmly sat on the horse's head until a neighbor came along and helped to get the harness untangled.

When motors displaced horses on the Ewen farm, Leila learned to operate tractors and trucks as well as cars. The first time she ever drove a car, she simply borrowed a key from the garageman and took off; she and her mother went to visit neighbors while the Ewen boys were at work in the fields.

A goal which Mrs. Ewen attained for each of her children was a college education. Leila attended the State Normal School at Mayville, and did her first teaching in a Traill County one-room rural school. After earning two degrees at Columbia University, she taught a summer term at Valley City State Teachers College.

In 1928 she came to Minot State Teachers College where her work has brought recognition and acclaim from educators, the warm gratitude of hundreds of rural teachers and thousands of farm boys and girls who have benefitted from her generous ministrations in their rural schools.

Early in her crusade for better teaching in the little white

Photo by courtesy of
Minot State Teachers College

Miss Leila C. Ewen

prairie schools, Miss Ewen inaugurated *in-service* training aimed to help the teacher to improve classroom procedures. Approximately fifty rural teachers in northwestern North Dakota annually enroll for this training. To bring this service to the schools, Miss Ewen travels about 25,000 miles each year.

During the winter months, she keeps her car stocked for possible emergency housekeeping on a storm-blocked road. On the back seat there will be canned soup, canned heat, candy bars, cheese, crackers, flares, a lantern, a supply of kerosene, a horsehide robe, stadium boots, extra coats, mittens and scarves, and a sleeping bag. On occasion a storm-bound schoolteacher has been the recipient of this emergency food.

Once, heading out of White Earth Valley in a March snow storm, she guided her car by the weeds that marked the edge of the road. She managed to reach Stanley where she hastily got her car into a garage, then phoned the railway station about a train she could hear whistling. It would pull out in five more minutes, she was informed.

In knee-deep snow, she made her way to the station in time to get aboard the caboose of a cattle train — the last train to move on the Great Northern tracks for several days. A six-hour ride and the lady professor was safely home at Minot.

Teachers who enroll for on-the-job training are entitled to a number of half-day visitations from Miss Ewen, or her assistant, Miss Bertha Okland. When Miss Ewen arrives at a rural school — be it in McKenzie, Rolette, or Divide county — children commonly leave their playground games and run to meet her. She is usually able to greet each child by name, and to remember his special interests.

The teacher calls the school to order and the pupils take their seats; Miss Ewen finds an inconspicuous place and sits down with a supply of blank paper before her. As the classes proceed, she writes an informal analysis of methods used and results obtained. There are compliments for good teaching, commendation for improvements; where there is need for better techniques, she makes suggestions about what to do and how to do it.

The teacher is given one copy of this analysis; the county superintendent of schools receives a second; and a third one is placed in Miss Ewen's office at the College.

Leila Ewen has become a familiar figure in the fifteen counties to which she has brought *in-service* training. Sometimes the rural party line gets busy when a farmwife spots the State Teachers College car parked near the schoolhouse, and at four o'clock a group of mothers will arrive there with sandwiches, cake and coffee for a cozy visit with their champion of better rural education.

Her guidance of teachers in the rural schools that are affiliated with the College goes beyond curriculum requirements. She helps with programs which grow out of class work, with parties for parents and pupils, and with school organizations. She is ever alert in locating materials needed by youngsters for their school projects, or for some child's personal hobby. She manages little gifts to "her" schools — perhaps a book, a flag stand, a magazine subscription, or a box of candy to make festive some particular occasion.

Children greet her joyfully, recognize her as a personal friend. One time, exhorting a boy who was having difficulty with decimals, Miss Ewen said, "You have a good head on your shoulders. If you work carefully, you will get the right answer." The boy replied, "I can tell it's a long time since you took arithmetic!"

Representative of her influence in improving teaching in general is the story of a farmer's wife in the Tagus area. A former teacher recruited during the acute teacher shortage of World War II, the woman had become discouraged with the results of her efforts. Then she met Miss Ewen who gave her the personal encouragement she needed. The farm wife enrolled in Saturday and summer classes, driving 70 miles daily to the College. Often she had to bring with her a four-year old grandson left to her care. After considerable difficulty, but always bolstered by Miss Ewen's kind interest, this grandmother was graduated from the Standard Course, and became a fully-accredited and confident teacher.

A woman of high ethical standards and personal decorum, this associate professor of education permits no careless behavior or sloppy attire among the cadets she supervises in the rural schools affiliated with the College. Each school day the cars are lined up at the entrance ready to leave the campus at 7:30 a.m. and Miss Ewen's experienced eye quickly checks the necessary teaching materials. And the cadet teachers.

One of these appeared one day without hose. Miss Ewen inquired of her, "Where are your stockings?"

"Oh, it's warm today," replied the girl, "I won't need them."

The lady professor reached into her car, drew out a pair of extra hose and instructed, "Now you go into the building and put these on."

When the girl returned, fully dressed, Miss Ewen and her novices left for their day's work at the schools.

Miss Ewen has served as president of the North Dakota Education Association, and on the board of directors of the National Education Association. When the State Board of Teaching Scholarships in North Dakota was established in 1949, Governor Fred Aandahl appointed her executive secretary of the Board, a position she continues to hold.

One cloudy winter morning as she motored to one of the Teaching Scholarship conferences at Bismarck, she came to the top of a hill and found a score of cars stalled in the deep ruts ahead. Her own car was of low chassis; she knew she could not get around the cars.

She was due at the Capitol in an hour, but she parked her car there near a mailbox. Luckily a car with more clearance next came over the hill. It bore the headliners for an out-of-office political party, and they invited her to ride with them to Bismarck.

At the Capitol, Miss Ewen stepped into the State Highway Department office. She described the condition of the road, told where she had been forced to leave her State-owned car. After naming the political candidates who had come to her aid, she dropped the keys of her car upon the office counter, and hurried off to her conference.

When she was ready to leave, late that afternoon, her car was waiting for her in the parking lot on the Capitol grounds.

For twenty years, this quick-witted woman with the snapping brown eyes has traveled all over western North Dakota to speak at teachers' meetings, programs of Parent-Teacher Associations, and service clubs. The trips have netted every sort of incident.

Once at a teachers' institute, a young pedagog who thought he knew all the answers started to "smart off." After several of his interruptions, Miss Ewen remarked that she would gladly measure the I.Q. of any who wished to volunteer. The cocksure young man briskly stepped to the platform.

Miss Ewen then pulled a tape measure from her briefcase and proceeded to measure the distance from the young man's eyes to the edge of his well-oiled hair. The audience laughed appreciatively, and the young man with all the answers realized that he had learned something he had not known before.

Annually, in May, Miss Ewen gives a tea for faculty members and county superintendents. At one such recent occasion, she was suprised when a florist's delivery boy came offering her a box. Scarcely taking time to look at him, she said, "Oh, no, not here. That must belong upstairs."

"But where will I find Miss Irwin?" the boy asked.

"There's no one by that name here," she replied.

"But this is for a tea," he persisted.

The unassuming Miss Ewen was puzzled. Some one near her suggested, "Perhaps you should open it."

Then this lady who has traveled thousands of miles over unimproved roads in every kind of weather for the sake of prairie children, found in the box an orchid corsage and the message: "For Miss Ewen with appreciation and love from your teachers in the Affiliated Schools."

And one who had sat in her classroom many years earlier, murmured, "There will always be orchids in our hearts for Miss Ewen."

52 Rosemeade Lady

"TEACHER, if you'd draw us some pictures — we could color them and put them on those ugly walls!"

Before Miss Laura Taylor could reply to the child, other pupils in the back-country rural school chorused, "Oh, yes, Teacher, we'd like to color pictures!"

Reluctantly, this young lady — destined to be, in 1952, the recipient of an award from the American Artists Professional League for her outstanding work as an artist — answered them, "But I don't know *anything* about drawing pictures!"

The eager smiles vanished at the teacher's words. As Laura Taylor looked at the boys and girls, she felt she had failed them — and resolved that next summer, she would go to Normal School and learn something about drawing.

At Valley City Normal, she was surprised to find that her art courses opened a fascinating new world. She first got her hands into clay in an elementary modeling class. One of her first pieces of clay sculpturing was a model of a kangaroo. It was far from perfect, but for Laura Taylor there was delight in the making of it. And that fall when she was back to teach, her pupils held it in their hands and treasured it.

She brought clay to school, and showed eager little hands how to form simple saucers and vases. She taught the children how to draw pictures, and saw their eyes shine when their crayoned handiwork brightened the schoolroom walls.

But one day, an irate grandmother, rapping sharply at the door, stood at the school threshold.

"I don't want my boys to be artists and poets," she shouted at Miss Taylor, "I want you should learn them reading and writing and 'rithmetic."

As graciously as she could, the teacher invited the objecting patron into the schoolroom, and tactfully showed her the latest course of study issued by the State Department of Public Instruction. Instructions therein clearly outlined required art work, picture study, lists of poetry to read and to memorize. Grandma was first incredulous, then dismayed.

"Well, if they got such crazy laws in North Dakota," she sputtered, "I don't s'pose there's nothing I can do about it!"

As she turned to leave, she caught sight of a mounted collection of free-hand drawings of North Dakota animals. Pointing to the likeness of a familiar but ill-famed creature, she snorted contemptuously, "Drawing skunks, too, yet!" and slammed the door.

It was at a summer session at Valley City that Glen Lukens, a visiting art professor from California, opened to Laura Taylor the enchanting field of pottery-making. Once she plunged her hands into resilient clay, she knew that here was the medium by which she would capture beauty.

Further years of teaching and sessions at the Valley City college followed. Graduating from the Standard Course during the depression, Laura Taylor found that art teachers were not in demand.

So, in 1932, she enrolled at the University of North Dakota and for the next three years took special work in art and ceramics. It was at the University that she first saw pottery formed on the potter's wheel. When her instructor, Julia Mattson, gave the class a demonstration and Laura Taylor saw the whirling lump of clay grow into a hollow and graceful vase, she laughed in sheer ecstasy.

The following year, Professor W. E. Budge, then head of the ceramics department, offered her part-time employment, and she was thus given opportunity to learn some of the practical aspects of pottery manufacture. She began to wish for a pottery plant of her own.

That same year she was given her first bit of recognition when a donkey she had modeled was accepted for display by the Robineau Memorial Exhibit at Syracuse, New York. The

Laura Taylor Hughes at the potter's wheel

next summer a ceramic tile picture she designed and completed at the University was shown in the North Dakota building at the *Century of Progress Exposition* in Chicago.

Following her work at the University, Miss Taylor taught primary grades for one year at Menoken, then was placed in supervision of a WPA federal clay project in western North Dakota. After three years with this project, she was selected as a pottery demonstrator at the *World of Tomorrow Exposition* in New York, and there spent seven happy months working at the potter's wheel six hours a day. Thousands of people watched her as she deftly shaped the clay, and over and over again she heard the remark (usually by some elderly gentleman much pleased with his own wit): "I bet you made mud pies when you were a little girl!" There were other more rewarding comments like that of a sweet old lady: "Making pottery is as lovely as making music!"

One day a visitor introduced himself as Robert J. Hughes of Wahpeton, North Dakota, and reminded her that he had once corresponded with her about his ambition to start a pottery plant in North Dakota — a plant that would utilize North Dakota clays. Hughes told her that Professor Budge had recommended her as having the necessary skill and knowledge for such an endeavor. Now would she go into partnership with Hughes at Wahpeton?

In January, 1940, Miss Taylor came to Wahpeton and began to work with Mandan clay in the back room of the Globe Gazette Printing Company building. A tin shed behind the building housed a kiln. In that back room and makeshift shed, Laura Taylor originated the Rosemeade Pottery that is now nationally famous.

Rosemeade Pottery flourished from the beginning, and a modern plant was soon built for its manufacture. World War II brought a shortage of glaze materials and of skilled help. By 1942 only women and boys were available. That same year there was an epidemic of weddings — five of the young women employees becoming brides. This matrimonial contagion spread into the executive offices of Rosemeade Pottery, and

Laura Taylor married the man whose first proposal — over coffee and doughnuts at a food stand on the New York fairgrounds — was a pottery plant in North Dakota using North Dakota clay and North Dakota designs.

The bridegroom was drafted as kiln fireman, and Mrs. Hughes crawled into the kilns to stack the glazed ware for firing. Eventually, conditions eased. Mr. Howard Lewis was obtained as plant manager, and the plant was enlarged. Today, nearly a thousand pieces of Rosemeade Pottery are manufactured daily at the Wahpeton plant.

Starting with an initial model of the State Capitol, the Rosemeade line has grown until it numbers close to 250 designs. Proved the most popular of them is the Chinese ring-necked pheasant. That one was first suggested by a salesman, and Mrs. Hughes designed a pair of pheasant salt and pepper shakers, expecting the sale of them to be primarily in South Dakota. But the pheasant shakers were so popular that Mrs. Hughes modeled pheasants in plaques, figures and vases.

Second piece of Rosemeade Pottery was a model of the world's largest register book kept at Chahinkapa Park in Wahpeton. (The book itself measures 58 by 33 inches, closed, and is 9 inches thick. Having space for a million signatures, it weighs 507 pounds. Leather-bound, beautifully-tooled, it was produced by the Globe-Gazette Printing Company and presented to the Park by Mr. Hughes.)

In response to requests from different localities, the Rosemeade lady has created pottery depicting the mallards and wall-eyed pike of Minnesota, Rocky Mountain goats of western parks, turkeys for the National Turkey Federation, pandas for Chicago's Brookfield Zoo, flamingoes and alligators for Florida shops.

To create a piece of Rosemeade Pottery, Mrs. Hughes first makes the original model from a lump of clay. From this original model, a number of hollow plaster molds are made.

The clay for reproducing the original model is prepared by soaking in water, then is strained through a fine sieve. This liquid clay is called "slip."

The dry plaster mold is filled with slip and allowed to stand until a layer of clay solidifies sufficiently to adhere to the inside of the mold. The rest of the clay slip is poured out, and a hollow cast piece is the result. Removed from the mold, this cast piece is left to dry for about 24 hours. It is then given its "bisque" firing in the kiln at 1600 degrees Fahrenheit.

Taken from the kiln, the piece is cooled. Next, the glaze is applied — by dipping or spraying or brushing — and the piece is returned to the kiln for a second firing, this time at 2050 degrees. Then it comes from the kiln, a lustrous piece of finished pottery.

In recognition of her outstanding contributions as an artist, Mrs. Hughes — together with Einar Olstad, the Sentinel Butte rancher-artist — was presented the North Dakota art award by the American Artists Professional League. Because of the superior work done by these two citizens, North Dakota received an honor roll citation in 1951, and the name of the state was engraved on the silver urn displayed by the League at its meetings — in 1952 — in New York City.

Laura Taylor Hughes' remarkable career began back in that rural school when she resolved that for her pupils' sake she must go to college and learn some art. The bread she cast upon the waters has returned after many days, for it is true as one five-year-old girl concluded as she watched the Rosemeade lady at the potter's wheel: "I'll bet this is your favorite work."

53 Ole, the Hermit

IN a small Valley City house lives an elderly man and a big green-eyed cat named Bertha. Although Ole Olson is known as "Ole, the Hermit" he has far too many callers to qualify as a recluse. This man's guest book has signatures of people from all over America, from several European countries, from Africa, the Philippines and the Hawaiian Islands.

It was in Norway that Ole, in 1882, was born. He was not a year old when his parents came to this land and settled in Dakota Territory. Ole, grown and married, was a Litchville farmer for about forty years. Retired, and alone, he bought the little place in Valley City and busied himself with whittling the quaint figures that have made him widely known as an artisan.

In Ole's "front room" are displayed many of his early carvings. On a window ledge is a burly "Dakota Squaw," her fists defiantly deep in her apron pockets. Close by is long-bearded "Old Adam." In a corner is a group portraying the flight of the Holy Family to Egypt. (Ole has included an angel — intent on hustling along the donkey.)

Ole seems to have a liking for whittling donkeys. At Litchville one time, after enjoying a soft ball game in which players were on donkeys, he carved the whole scene — players and spectators.

Ole long ago gave up the attempt to fill all demands for his figurines. He frequently is set back by illness. An infected hand once interrupted his work. True artist that he is, he is indifferent to the increasing popularity of his product. And the same is true of his skill's meaning in dollars. For, when one

"Ole the Hermit"

of Chicago's largest department stores offered Ole an attractive salary for the simple job of sitting and whittling for throngs of shoppers to behold, his response was the indignant snort, "What you think I am? A monkey in a cage?"

Life in the little house with green-eyed Bertha's contented purring conforms more to Ole's notion of what is the good life than does an abundance of big-town luxuries and laudation. Here he can whittle at will, can visit with his neighbors and chat with those who come in hope of getting him to whittle something for them.

The typical "Ole, the Hermit" figurine is a mirth-provoking one, and most often it depicts an oldster — a chin-whiskered man with baggy trousers, or a grandma in a shawl. A subject that has been especially popular is an old couple out fishing: the man, upright in the front of the boat, has just made a cast and has caught himself — in the seat of his pants; he registers proper humiliation and his wife, disgust.

Ole's formula for carving amusing figures is as simple as his mode of living: "You just take a piece of wood. You look at it. You imagine what you want. Then you just cut away the wood you don't want."

54 Whittler of Birds

THOMAS Hansen of Valley City is one of those who, because of a disability, discovered and developed a talent.

Stricken with osteo-mylitis at the age of twelve, Tom was hospitalized for a long time, then spent many months in a wheel chair. Time hung heavy on his hands, and out of sheer boredom, he began to whittle aimlessly.

But Tom's whittling found direction through one of his dominant interests — hunting and fishing. Always a wild life enthusiast, he observed the migration of waterfowl each season, and became much interested in the identification and habits of the many game birds of his locality. As he gained facility with his whittling, he naturally turned to these birds for his models.

He whittled only occasionally during the years when he farmed for a living. But when he retired and came to Valley City to live, he had more time to spend with his knife. He gave his carved birds to friends and relatives who proudly displayed them to their friends — and Tom Hansen soon found himself in a growing business.

So realistically carved and painted are Hansen's birds that game wardens buy models they can use when lecturing. Youth and wild life groups use Hansen's handiwork to help teach the identification of game birds.

Tom makes his birds in pairs because the male and female of each species are usually very different in color and feather pattern. Producing a dozen of each at a time, he first draws the pattern, traces it upon a piece of pine or basswood, cuts the outline on a jig saw, carves it into form with a jackknife, then sands and paints.

These bird models are prized decorations in many North Dakota homes and they are also to be found in such faraway places as Palestine, Egypt, Alaska and several European countries.

Vice president of the North Dakota Wildlife Association, Hansen continues to be a hunting and fishing enthusiast. In his home he has a collection of guns and cartridges, and a number of birds which he has mounted. But it is his exhibit of carved birds that elicits the most fervent exclamations of admiration, and seldom can a visitor leave Tom Hansen's home without first purchasing a pair of Hansen's birds for his own home.

Thomas Hansen, hunter,
beams over a trophy

A display of birds carved by
Thomas Hansen

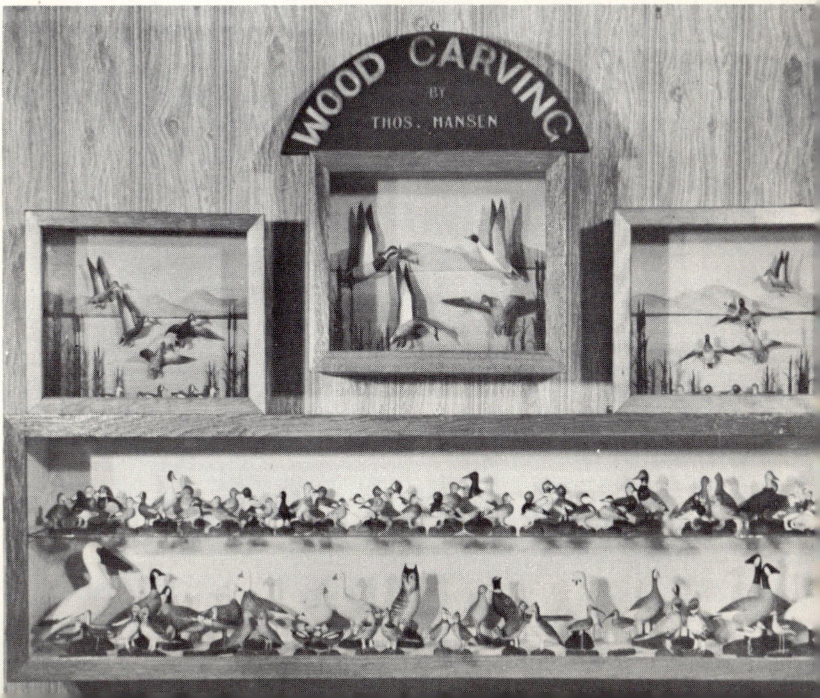

55 Indomitable Artist

THIS is the story of an artist who draws her pictures with a pencil held in her mouth.

When she was a sophomore in the Valley City high school, Grace Layton won first place in the North Dakota Easter Seal design contest. By graduation time — 1949 — she had elected art as her college major.

On a PEO scholarship, she entered Cottey Junior College for Women at Nevada, Missouri. Here was a year of happiness! For as she, under guidance, progressed in drawing and design, the delight in her chosen field expanded.

Three weeks after she came home to Valley City for the summer vacation, she was taken ill with dread poliomyelitis — rushed to St. Luke's Hospital in Fargo and kept for months in a respirator. In January, 1951, when breathing without the "iron lung" was possible, she was transferred to Sheltering Arms Hospital at Minneapolis.

While there had been some improvement in her condition, she was still almost completely paralyzed. The girl who wanted to be an artist could not lift a finger.

She asked the attending physician if she could be taken to the occupational therapy department — she would like to try drawing. The doctor was sure she could do no drawing — after all, she could move only her head.

But the indomitable girl persisted in her request until the doctor agreed to let her have a try at it.

That same day, then, the occupational therapist taped a charcoal pencil to the end of a stick, and placed the stick in Grace Layton's mouth. With a drawing board adjusted in a favorable position, the determined girl was ready for a "try at it."

She gripped the stick between her teeth and started to experiment. As she drew the first wavering lines, a fierce hope rose in her. And great was her joy the day she could show an easily-recognized figure to the kind and helpful therapist.

After eight months at Sheltering Arms, Grace was discharged. A short time later, she spent four months at Georgia Warm Springs Foundation.

Then she came home again — home to family and neighbors and friends whose compassion could never bring back to her the use of her arms and legs. Ahead of Grace Layton stretched the adult years that once had beckoned with such high promise. No one could have blamed her had she resigned herself to a bleak, hopeless, helpless invalid's life.

But Grace resolved that, by a pencil in her mouth, she would learn to support herself. Her first Christmas at home she drew her own greetings cards, and the friends who received them were enthusiastic.

Encouraged, she drew four teen-age girl designs: a girl golfing, one gardening, one riding a surfboard, and the other square dancing. These she had lithographed on notepaper and packaged as "Vacation Notes."

No sooner, though, was the initial run of notepaper printed than uncertainty assailed Grace. Would the four teen-agers appeal to a public provided with such extensive choice in personal stationery — all the work of experts? Might it not well be that the lot of expensively produced sheets be, finally, utilized to paper the walls of her own room?

A few weeks, only, and she had the answer. Mail orders came as a result of sample boxes sent to interested friends in different parts of the country. The friends first, then the boxes themselves, became Grace Layton's salesmen — and the orders rapidly increased. It wasn't long before this indomitable artist knew that she would never use her notepaper for wallpaper.

After the success of "Vacation Notes," Grace prepared a set of Christmas card designs, and followed this with various notepaper assortments which eventually were to bring letters

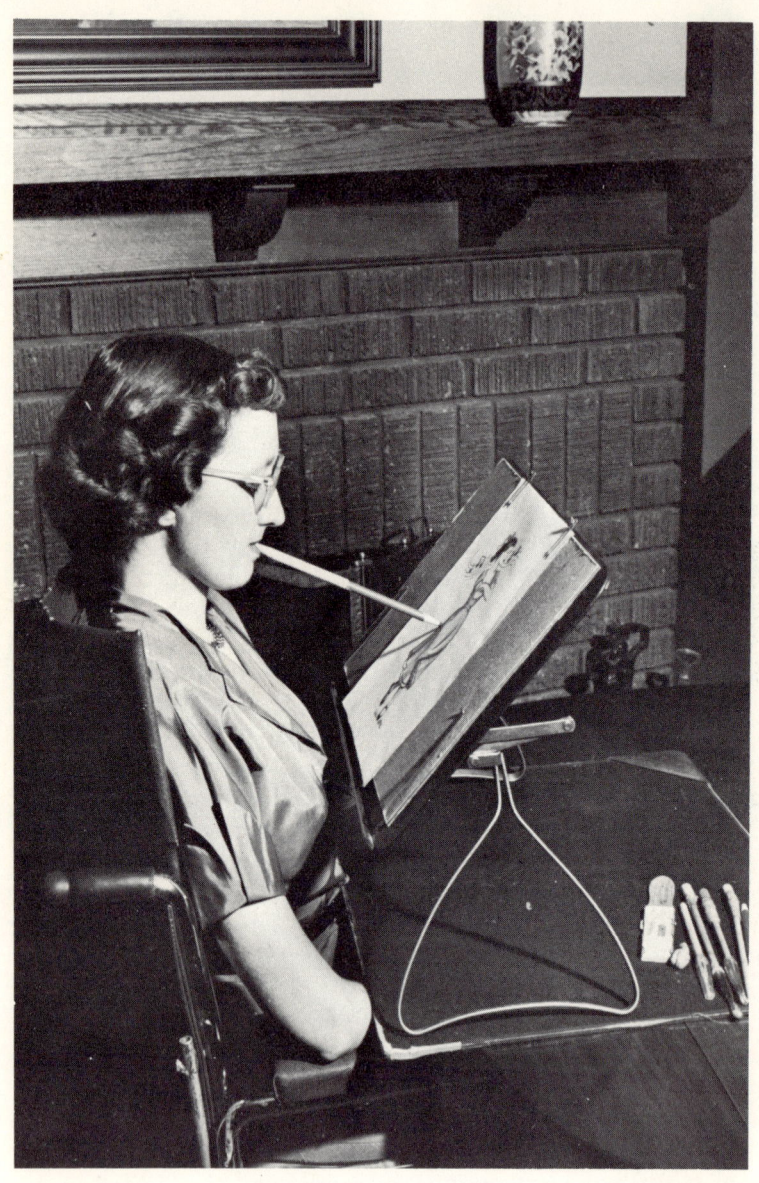

Grace Layton

and orders from every state in the Union — and some from Canada.

Eager to do something for the National Foundation for Infantile Paralysis — which had been of such great help to her — Grace designed and had printed each year a box of notepaper to be sold exclusively for the benefit of the March of Dimes. From the first two years of such sales, she was able to donate more than two thousand dollars to the Foundation.

As a girl, Grace found much delight in playing the piano. Now she must depend on others for her music. A large collection of classical recordings is the source of much enjoyment. Occasionally, as she is able to do so, she makes trips to Fargo and Minneapolis to attend plays and concerts.

A living reproach to able-bodied wards of charity, Grace Layton is not content merely to be a self-supporting American citizen. As conditions permit, she enrolls in art courses at the Valley City State Teachers College — for, again, the years ahead beckon with promise for this talented girl who cannot use her hands.

The spirit in her echoes the words of Robert Frost's doctor who, clucking his little horse on through the deep snow, says: "For I have promises to keep, and miles to go before I sleep."

56 Three Maids and a Mission

IN March, 1948, three young women set out over North Dakota prairies in a modern covered wagon. Over rural roads of dirt, gumbo and scoria they went. Intermittently and in verse, they kept a casual log of their doings. Their first lyric entry was:

> We have a clinic
> Sent out on wheels
> 'Round North Dakota
> By Easter Seals —
> With special gearing
> For speech and hearing —
> The Mobile Clinic.

For five years that Mobile Clinic traveled over the state — and the three young women lost but three days to the oftentimes inclement weather. After their experience in Pat Donan's "land of the golden grain" they were not in agreement with him that in North Dakota "all the breezes are trained to sing psalm-tunes in pianissimo style, and our wildest blizzards, as unenlightened downeasters sometimes term them, are used by gentle mothers to lull their babies to sleep." They penned their own opinion:

> In North Dakota
> I've heard 'em say
> That if a blizzard
> Is on the way,
> Before it dares come
> It gets permission from
> The Mobile Clinic.

The Mobile Unit and three staff members, l. to r., Misses Janet Smaltz, Marge Hurst, and Lucille Holtan. In the background is the Easter Seals headquarters building.

Miss Smaltz gives a rural youngster speech therapy in the Mobile Clinic trailer.

Miss Smaltz shovels a path for children to get into the Mobile Unit parked on a road at Reynolds in Traill County, winter of 1949.

"What's in there?"

On their first trip out, the three women left Easter Seal headquarters at Jamestown, and drove cautiously down Highway 10 in a heavy snowstorm. By bedtime, they were still 140 miles from their destination of Mott. They parked beside the gravel road and got into the trailer. Stiff from cold, they lay down to rest — all their clothes on, blankets over them, the trailer stove going full blast. At 6 next morning, breakfastless, they resumed their way, wondering dismally how many such frigid nights their mission held for them. While breakfasting in a warm hotel, they heard by radio report, that, in the night, the temperature had dropped to 28 below zero.

During the winter months, the three became accustomed to wearing boots all day — "and right up to the edge of the bed, then pop into them first thing in the morning. The fact that we pried them off the floor in the morning warned us that our feet might be chilly for another day." They learned to eat frozen corned beef sandwiches, to wash in ice water, and dress in 20 below weather.

Yet they seldom had a cold. Doubtless the reason for this immunity was the "Toe Box" that they invented. This was a cardboard carton fitted with a heating pad.

Once during hours of struggle to get the trailer out of deep mud, they got so thoroughly soaked that by common reasoning, they *"should* have taken pneumonia." The necessity of wearing several layers of heavy clothing during the most frigid weather taught them to esteem the "wonderful luxury of warmth." Their trailer life added to the log:

The other night
We went to town;
Lulu, excited,
Jumped up and down —
The running water,
It really got her,
'Cause we ain't had none.
We saw a movie,
And we ate ice cream;

Marge was excited,
Like in a dream.
We took our boots off —
Even our coats off!
And had a swell time!

Director of the Mobile Clinic party was Miss Janet M. Smaltz. The two working with her were Miss Marge Hurst, speech therapist, and Miss Lucille Holtan, assistant. They lived and worked in a 20 by 7½ foot trailer and shortly learned "the beauty of spacious living," for they shared trailer space with a davenport-bed, a folding canvas cot, an oil burner, 6 folding chairs, a 100-volume professional library, 2 audiometers, a tape recorder, a disc recorder, a large office file, 2 typewriters and typewriter tables, hearing aids, miscellaneous therapy equipment, batteries, 2 fire extinguishers, an electric plate, dishes for 4, cupboards and closets to contain groceries, cooking utensils and clothing.

For nine months of the school year, the three maids drove about the state to fulfill their mission of finding children with speech and hearing difficulties. They tested more than 28,000 children (every school child in eleven counties) and found 6.9 per cent needing speech therapy, another 5.5 requiring medical attention because of hearing losses.

Until the Mobile Clinic provided them, there were no statistics available as to the needs of speech and hearing facilities for North Dakota school children. Subsequent legislation provided a testing and therapy program to be administered through the public schools, and the Mobile Clinic was changed to a referral type service.

When the Mobile Unit parked near a rural school, the staff members and their equipment were the objects of much avid curiosity. As they unhitched, and got the trailer electric cord connected with the school's nearest outlet (if such there was), school children would gather about to ask, "What's in there? Do we get to come in? Does it hurt? What is *that* thing?" Many times *"that* thing" was the sponge rubber duck decoy fastened just above the trailer door to provide more gentle impact when some tall person attempted exit.

At one school, where the Mobile Unit had arrived before daylight, the pupils lined up at a respectful distance to view the strange parked vehicle. The three trailer inhabitants were eating breakfast at the time, and as one of them arose from the table, there were excited shouts from the children outside, "I seen one! I seen one!"

Once after driving 420 miles — between 3:00 p.m. and 3:00 a.m. — in circumventing a flooded area, the Mobile Clinic girls were so exhausted, they felt like cancelling the day's appointments. But in that single day's testing, they found three children with severe speech defects and badly in need of the help later given them.

For Janet Smaltz and her co-workers, the journeying over North Dakota became a "saga of mud, sweat, and lefse." Of mud and gumbo, there was too much; and unladylike sweat resulted from shoveling snow and working in mud to get the trailer through on unimproved roads.

But the "lefse," that was a different matter. That betokened the hospitality of prairie hearts: the tendered quart of cream, carton of fresh eggs, warm bed, warm meal; and, too, the gratitude expressed by many ranchers, farmers, and small town people who appreciated the conscientious ministry of three young women who turned their backs upon creature comforts and conveniences so that they might be of service to the children of North Dakota. The end reaction of the three — expressed in their log's idiom and rhyme — was:

> *But city life ain't*
> *For us no more;*
> *We can't sit still like*
> *We did before;*
> *It's our devotion*
> *That keeps in motion*
> *The Mobile Clinic.*

57 Champion of the Shackled

ONE of the most challenging people in North Dakota is Dr. Anne H. Carlsen, superintendent of The Crippled Children's School at Jamestown.

Anne Carlsen was born at Grantsburg, Wisconsin on a bleak November night. When the attending physician, Dr. E. I. Bunker, returned to his home he was too dispirited to respond to his wife's greeting, for the child he had delivered had only stubs of arms terminating above the elbow, a right leg that was only a short, dangling end, and the left deformed and clubfooted.

The next morning he told his wife about the Carlsen baby, and Mrs. Bunker exclaimed, "Oh, how terrible! Will she live?"

Then fiercely he replied, "Of course she will live. She has as much right to live as any one. Who can tell — she may become an intellectual prodigy, she may prove a greater blessing to humanity than most of us who do have arms and legs!"

Grantsburg townsfolks wept in compassion not only for the child but also for her parents. But Alfred and Maren Carlsen tucked the helpless infant into the bosom of their love, and resolved that she would be given every opportunity to live a full and happy life.

When Anne was four years old, her mother died, and the mantle of motherhood fell over the slight shoulders of her sister Clara, then thirteen years old. Four brothers stood by to help the little sister who could do little more than melt hearts with her winsome smile. That smile won many friends, a few of whom often came early in the morning to help Clara dress Anne for another carefree day.

Specimen of
Dr. Anne Carlsen's
"arm-writing"

The Crippled Children's School
Jamestown, North Dakota

Office of the Superintendent
Anne H. Carlsen, Ph. D.

August 16, 1954

Dear Bill,

Your last letter was a most welcome one. Congratulations! Getting that first job is a real accomplishment. All of us here at the school are rejoicing with you for we know that you can put your hard

Our
fill

Dr. Anne H. Carlsen at her desk at The Crippled Children's School, Jamestown

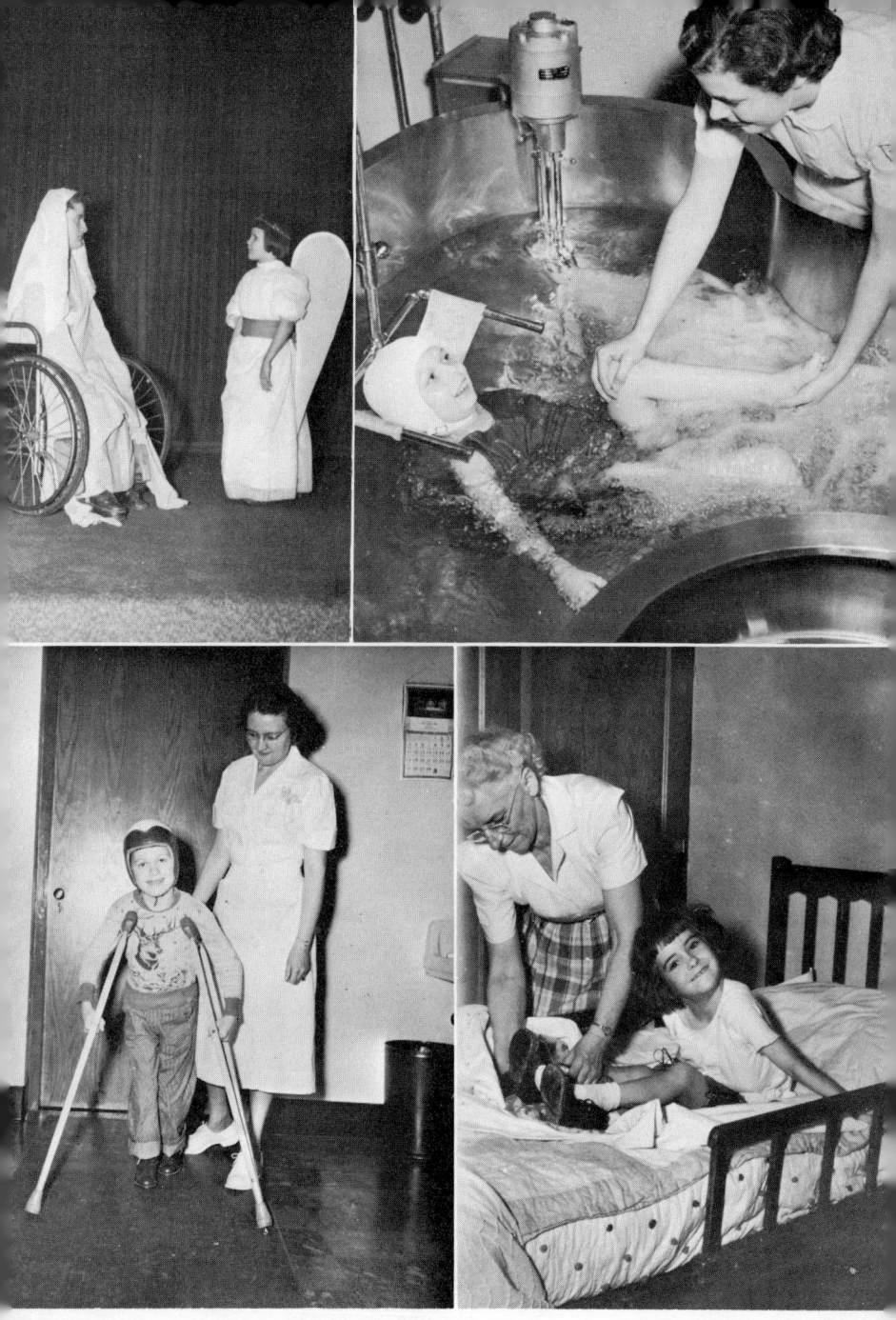

Scenes at The Crippled Children's School, Jamestown

There was always something going on at the Carlsen home, and the backyard was a favorite gathering place for Grantsburg children. So Anne had many playmates.

Gay-hearted, high-spirited, she delighted in taking part in neighborhood games. She early learned to propel her strong young body over the ground so she could join in Pum-Pum-Pullaway and Prisoner's Base. When the game was baseball, special rules went into effect for Anne so that bases were shortened for her, or other children at bases walked instead of running.

After she got her kiddie car, her speed increased. She could sit on it, steer it with her little arm-stubs, shove it along with the one awkward foot. Seldom, though, had she need to propel herself, for there was always one of the brothers or a playmate eager to push the kiddie-car for her.

Yet it was not like having legs. While she did not mind so much the lack of hands, little Anne longed for legs so that she could *run* — legs that could scamper across sidewalks and speed away in a game of tag with her nimble-footed playmates. Her staunch friend, Dr. Bunker, fitted her with an artificial leg, but it was not successful—Anne went back to the kiddie car.

When she was eight years old, she was allowed to attend public school the last two months of the term. Her sister and brothers had already taught her a little reading, and she found school fascinating as the great, wide world of books began opening for her its immeasurable treasure.

"Two arms and two legs missing aren't as important as one head present," Alfred Carlsen would encourage his daughter. "Best way to make that head help the most, though, is to get it educated."

In the fall, Anne entered school, and she passed both first and second grades that term. She spent her ninth year at Wisconsin General Hospital where, through surgery, the contractures of her knee were straightened, though the leg remained weak. Anne came home, able to walk by means of a clumsy device which, when used, did not permit her to sit down. She took her meals standing up until her brothers taught her to spread the contraption over the old kiddie car. But she soon discarded the device, and depended on the kiddie car and a coaster wagon for transportation.

Back at school again, she averaged two grades a year; so, at twelve, she was ready for high school. One of the most memorable incidents of Anne's grade school days happened when a boy was pushing her at boy-speed down the school hallway. She wasn't able to steer the kiddie car too well when she turned lickity-cut into her classroom, so she drove smack over her teacher's toes.

With Anne's interest in mind, Alfred Carlsen moved his family to St. Paul and located them within a block of St. Paul Luther Academy; he obtained work as a gardener at Gillette Hospital.

Her freshman year at Luther Academy was one of the unhappiest times of Anne's life. She was away from the bulwark of love and acceptance that had surrounded her in the Grantsburg village. Now she was among strangers who stared at her, and caused her to realize how severely handicapped she was, how tragically "different" she was from her able-bodied schoolmates. But, bolstered by her family's love, by the kindness of her teachers and of the school head, the Reverend W. F. Schmidt, Anne learned to hurdle the bleak realizations and to live once more in her high spirit. Gradually, she made a new circle of friends, and school studies took on zest again.

In her junior year, she was again hospitalized. The left leg was amputated just below the knee. Fitted with artificial legs, Anne returned to school, able to walk with the aid of crutches.

She earned her high school diploma, completed two years of junior college work at the Academy. She then transferred to the University of Minnesota, hoping there to get training that would make her self-supporting.

Always, she had wanted to teach school. The University's department of education, however, discouraged her in this. In those depression years, she was reminded of the surplus of teachers — able-bodied teachers.

So she consulted Dr. E. G. Williamson, head of the University counselling bureau, and thereby became one of his "problems." She told him that if teaching was out of the question, she would like to do library work. But the library department instructors pointed out that she would be unable to carry books up and down stairs. Her aptitude tests showed that she had ability in literary composition, so Williamson suggested that she consider creative writing.

Anne Carlsen graduated from the liberal arts college with a major in composition and English. Her sheepskin, however, brought her no job. When her family offered to finance further study, she returned to the University for courses in journalism.

That winter, her beloved father died. Anne quit school, went to live with her sister Clara who was now married. Half-heartedly, Anne undertook to write for a living. Her brothers bought her a typewriter. For her stubs of arms, they made leather cuffs, fastening to each cuff a rubber tipped metal finger. Anne punched out a number of manuscripts, sent them out to editors, but garnered only rejection slips.

She did baby-sitting, read a great deal. On hearing that a Minneapolis church publishing house hired handicapped people, she decided to apply for a position as proof reader. She wrote to the Reverend Schmidt, asking if he would recommend her to the publishing company.

Schmidt hastened to assure her that he would gladly do so, but asked her if she would not prefer teaching school to reading proof. He told her a teacher was needed at a school for crippled children located at Fargo, North Dakota, and that he had already recommended her for the position.

Anne was so excited over the possibility of teaching that she at once telephoned the Reverend W. B. Schoenbohn, director of the Good Samaritan School in Fargo. He requested a personal interview. Anne was soon hired. Her pay was to be 25 dollars a month, with board and room provided at the School.

The size of her pay check was not of major importance to Anne Carlsen; what mattered was that she could serve in her preferred field and be, at the same time, self-supporting.

She now followed the routine of teaching at the School, and attending summer sessions either at the University of Minnesota or the State College of Education, Greeley, Colorado until she had earned her Master's degree in education.

When, in 1940, the School was moved to Jamestown, she worked as a bedside instructor at Gillette Hospital, St. Paul. The following five years she served as high school teacher at the School — now known as The Crippled Children's School — then took two years' leave of absence to work on her doctorate. She was awarded her Ph.D. in education by the University of Minnesota, June, 1949, and the next year was appointed superintendent of the School.

Dr. Anne Carlsen chuckles now when she relates how the Wisconsin state psychologist examined her during her first year at grade school and pronounced her "educable." But there is fervency in her voice when she speaks of the hundreds of handicapped youngsters who, likewise, are capable of being educated but are not given opportunity to develop their potentialities.

The school she superintends is supported by voluntary contributions. Each year this school trains severely handicapped young people to arise from Sloughs of Despond and to go — some walking, some always in wheelchairs — into that Promised Land that most of us take for granted, the Promised Land of economic and social independence.

Many of the students, like Dr. Carlson, have been born crippled in some way. Others have been injured in accidents or are the victims of polio or arthritis. But whatever the cause or the condition, the boys and girls soon realize that in this quick-smiling superintendent they have a staunch champion, a friend who is daily proof of what it is possible for them also to accomplish.

"The spirit is a wonderful thing," this fair, blue-eyed superintendent will tell you. "All of us here know what it can do."

Anne Carlsen's "arm-writing" is more legible than the script most of us do with good hands and fingers. On her many speaking engagements, she regularly travels alone, and goes by plane, bus or train. Her hosts are amazed at her ability to care for herself.

A healthy humor is one of her dominant traits. She belongs to a number of organizations, and she tells you, "When they pass the paper around for interested people to sign, I always think it is better to sign or folks will think I am unable to write." She is obliged to mount stairs backwards — "It is easier to fall that way." When she gets ready for a sleighride with teachers and students, she will say, "Better bring a blanket along for me so I can keep my feet warm."

Anne Carlsen's vibrant spirit will always keep her youthful. Again and again, some visitor at the School has asked, at sight of the superintendent coming down the hallway on her crutches: "What grade is *that* girl in?"

58 Lady Under the Sod

*O*NE of the few remaining sodhouse post offices in North Dakota is located at Fayette in Dunn County. A building of sod and gumbo walls and sodded roof, it was erected in 1900 by Frank Little and has since housed the post office and store in the tiny town tucked into the shelter of great sprawling hills.

To Fayette, Miss Anna Fisher came in 1905 and has remained since as postmistress and storekeeper in the enduring soddy. For nearly half a century now, she and her soddy have

The sod post office and store at Fayette

Leo D. Harris Photo

Miss Anna Fisher and a young friend stand before the postmistress' Model A. The soddy is in the background.

weathered drouth, hail, dust storm and blizzard — in temperatures ranging from 117 above zero to 40 below.

Winter snows cover the dirt roof with extra insulation against the cold; summer sun and rain green it with growing flowers, grasses and weeds. In spring the wild prairie rose is a-bloom on the roof, and in summer the sunflower. A season of drouth will bring a thatch of green Russian Thistle; always there is some sage brush.

A stone-walled house nearby is Miss Fisher's residence, but it is with the soddy that most folks thereabouts associate her. Under its sod roof, through years of plenty and years of dust and wind, she has sorted mail, sold stamps and groceries. She has been a sympathetic center for relaying messages among scattered neighbors, and in the early years frequently located the horse-and-buggy doctor and dispatched him to a bed of pain.

The feverish hurry, the dependence on commercial entertainment, the bustling to and fro — this is not Anna Fisher's way of life; she has learned the art of living happily with oneself. Isolating winter storms hold no fear for her; under the sod roof is snug comfort with a stove glowing from the heat of lignite coal and cherry wood. And many a prairie neighbor has found Anna Fisher's soddy a gracious haven during a sudden blizzard.

THE END